Praise for

BALANCE IS BULLSH*T

"With a combo of love, sass, compassion, and most importantly, moving heartfelt honesty from her own motherhood journey, Beach gives mommas permission to drop the Momma Perfection Obsession and the Super Momma capes that have worn us down and worn us out. In *Balance is Bullsh*t,* she helps mothers bring voice to what are often secret, unexpressed feelings of guilt or feelings of Momma Bondage, to understanding self-care—newly—and in a deeper way that is more personal and holistic, addressing a mother's whole self: emotionally, mentally, physically, socially, and spiritually."

—**Debrena Jackson Gandy,** author of *Sacred Pampering Principles, All the Joy You Can Stand,* and *The Love Lies*

BALANCE IS BULLSH*T

ELISHA BEACH

Health Communications, Inc.
Mt. Pleasant, SC

www.hcibooks.com

Library of Congress Cataloging-in-Publication Data
is available through the Library of Congress

ISBN-13: 978-0-7573-2550-2 (Paperback)
ISBN-10: 0-7573-2550-5 (Paperback)
ISBN-13: 978-0-7573-2551-9 (ePub)
ISBN-10: 0-7573-2551-3 (ePub)

Publisher: Health Communications, Inc.
1240 Winnowing Way, Suite 102
Mt. Pleasant, SC 29466

Cover, interior design, and formatting by Larissa Hise Henoch

To every mom
that has struggled to achieve
the ever elusive "balance" in her life

To the ones who made me the mom I am today . . .
Roarke, Tyler, Alex, Quincey, Ledgend,
Jackson, Nolan, and Davis

And to Mike,
the person who has been my
greatest support

CONTENTS

INTRODUCTION

HEY, MOMMA. How often do you hear the term "self-care"? *You need to practice more self-care, you have to take more time for self-care, self-care this, self-care that.* But I am going to guess that the term "self-care" has become for you an annoying buzzword more likely to invoke guttural moans, guffaws, and deep eye rolls instead of feelings of relief. Why? Because for so long, moms have been sold this ridiculous idea that we can balance it all and still prioritize our own needs—yet so many of us feel like we are constantly in survival mode just trying to make it through the day. We have limited time and little to no support and are constantly reminded of everything we aren't getting right.

It's no wonder the mere mention of self-care has become just another overwhelming thing for moms to add to their never-ending to-do list. It feels like toxic positivity masking another way to bully moms into feeling guilty because, yet again, we can't possibly live up to this preconceived idea of motherhood that society is ramming down our throats. It's become pretty clear that this balancing act that mothers have been sold is total bullshit! And I don't know about you, but I am fed up with it. I believe it's time that moms take back control of our own self-care.

I fell for the whole thing. I truly believed that I could be the best mom, be successful at my career, be a great wife, and make it all look easy. I thought if I had quiet time in the morning, worked out, got my nails done regularly, and ended my nights with a glass of wine or cup of tea, I should be able to handle all that was expected of me. And to my own detriment, I fought and fought and fought for that to be true. But damn, was I wrong. Instead, I was constantly fighting the feelings of exhaustion, failure, and overwhelm.

After parenting my way through almost two years of the hell that we know as the COVID pandemic (aka pure pandemonium), I broke. I didn't have a major meltdown or anything like that. One day, I woke up and I just couldn't anymore. I couldn't focus, I couldn't muster any energy, I couldn't summon a damn about anything, and I couldn't figure out why.

I usually come out of the holiday season rested and energized with a plan for the new year ready to go. As soon as my kids are back in school, normally I excitedly jump full force into everyday life as a mom, with work projects and a list of New Year's resolutions I plan to pursue. But this time, I was a broken, exhausted, and overwhelmed mess. I was far beyond my breaking point, and I didn't even have the capacity to see it coming because I was basically a zombie of a person. I tried so hard to pick myself up, but I just couldn't pull it together and move on. I realized I had once again fallen into the trap of thinking I could balance it all on my own, and I felt like I had failed miserably. Then I was diagnosed with clinical burnout.

What is that? It's a state of emotional, physical, and mental exhaustion resulting from prolonged or chronic stress that is recognized as a medical diagnosis by the World Health Organization. It often shows up as exhaustion, lack of motivation, self-alienation, and an inability to perform duties. So, even though "mommy burnout" is often joked about, there is actually a medical diagnosis for moms suffering from being chronically exhausted and stressed out.

I had no idea.

The sad part is, like so many other moms, I was pissed at myself and carried so much blame. I was pissed for missing the signs. I was pissed because the pandemic put me in a position where I didn't really have a choice. I was pissed that the schools shut down and I was responsible for four neurodivergent kids' virtual schooling and homeschooling and managing fifty-two zoom sessions a week while still maintaining my workload. I was pissed at my husband just because he had to work out of town. I was pissed because I felt like I had no choice but to keep going even though I knew I was falling apart at the seams. And, when it was "over," I was pissed at society for acting like I was supposed to pick up like the last two years of my life never happened and just move on like I wasn't right in the middle of a mental health crisis.

As I worked through eighteen months of therapy to get back to some version of myself, I had to ask, *How the hell did I get here?* I thought I had figured out this whole self-care thing. And I realized, it's not that I wasn't taking care of myself, I was just flat-out doing too much and did not have enough support for what I was going through. I had to learn that I don't have to be a superhero or self-sacrificing martyr to be a good mom, wife, friend, or daughter. In fact, I had to learn that the exact opposite is true.

You can't be the best version of yourself if your needs are constantly neglected while you take care of everyone else's. Yes, most of us manage most of the time, but eventually the stress bubbles over.

It's only a matter of time before you crash and burn, mommy brain kicks into full drive, and the next thing you know you are crying on the living room floor because you yelled at everybody, you can't find your keys or your cell phone, you are running late, and you feel like you are failing at balancing everything.

Every time I see an interview with a woman who happens to be a mother, the question always asked is "How do you balance it all?" I used to listen attentively for the answer, thinking that surely *this* person had figured out some way to make it all work. And now, every time I hear that question, I can feel rage bubbling up from the depths of my soul because that question perpetuates the nonsense idea that mothers have discovered some magical answer somehow making them capable of doing it all—when the truth is, it's impossible to balance it all, all the time. Mothers are no more capable than anyone else, yet we are constantly being held to unrealistic standards.

Let me ask you: Are you always doing for others but never have time to prioritize your needs? Does it seem like your to-do list is on permanent scroll? Are you feeling perpetually burned out with no relief in sight? Does it feel like you can never get it all right no matter what you do or how hard you try?

What if I told you it's not you? You are not failing.

Momma, we have been sold a bunch of bullshit. Society made us believe that motherhood would be the most natural role to transition into, that sacrificing yourself is the definition of a good mother, and putting everyone else's needs first is a requirement of your role in the household. And worst of all, you should be able to easily balance all that comes along with this journey of motherhood, including caring for your own needs.

Who Am I to Have an Opinion About This?

I am not a therapist or some self-care guru. I am the birth mom of three kids, the adoptive mom of one, and the stepmom of four. Yep, you did the math right. I've been and still am parenting eight kids in one capacity or another. I have been there, done that, and cried about it in my closet. I've navigated working, staying at home, taking care of children with major medical situations, IEPs, 504s, blended families, family court, caring for an elderly parent, and so much more. I have run myself ragged, lost myself in motherhood, and burned out multiple times. I finally realized if I planned to survive motherhood, I had to figure out how to make the space I need for me in my life.

You and I have all been sold the dream that we can raise kids like a stay-at-home mom while bringing in income to contribute. We can easily keep a clean, organized home and make healthy, homemade dinners. We can raise well-rounded, kind, high-achieving kids by way of society-approved, positive, responsive, nonauthoritative parenting techniques in a stress-free, ever-joyous environment. There is time for each kid to participate in a sport and learn a musical instrument, and you should attend every practice, performance, and game. And don't forget to keep up with grades, homework, and reading—and monitoring all online activity and device usage.

You *should* be able to manage the household and maintain everyone's schedule and still make time for yourself. Be a "good" wife, dutiful daughter, dependable friend, and contributing member of your community (i.e., volunteer for the PTA, HOA, church activities, and neighborhood watch), but set personal boundaries on your time. Oh, and don't forget to get eight hours of sleep, work out on a regular basis, eat healthy, maintain societal beauty standards, drink the recommended amount of water, attend therapy, sustain friendships, accomplish personal goals, and keep up with hobbies. No big deal, right? (Insert maniacal, exhausted laugh followed by a sob session.) Well, I am not buying this dream anymore and I call *bullshit!*

What This Book's About

It doesn't matter if you are a working mom, crunchy mom, married mom, stay-at-home mom, adoptive mom, tiger mom, single mom, work-at-home mom, helicopter mom, divorced mom, homeschooling mom, part-time working mom, stepmom, sports mom, silky mom, hot-mess mom, or whatever random combination of mom. Every last one of us is struggling to balance it all. I can almost guarantee that most of us have tried reading a self-care book or two, but so many of the so-called self-care books don't deal with the reality of real-life, day-to-day motherhood. They tell you all the things you should be doing but not how the hell to actually accomplish any of it while trying your best to navigate the impossible list of expectations that come with being a mom.

I am assuming if you picked up this book, you feel the same way. You know that you need to focus on taking better care of yourself, but you are struggling with the when, where, what, and how the hell anyone is incorporating self-care into this chaotic life. You have probably watched a ton of self-care gurus on social media, and maybe you rolled your eyes at their perfectly curated morning routine or guffawed at their seemingly child-free, ultraclean home.

I wrote this book to give everyday moms practical advice from another mom who gets it. This book is designed to help you take ownership of your self-care and build a self-care practice that supports *you* in prioritizing *your* needs, for *your* life, with *your* circumstances, and can ebb and flow as *your* life changes. This book helps you come to terms with the reality of your life as a mother, prioritize self-care practices that are important to you, get over mom guilt and Super Mom Syndrome, and build a modern-day village to support you in your journey. I definitely throw in a few good rants (because a good fucking rant is often needed) but also remind you to celebrate your wins and give yourself grace.

You don't have to fulfill the role of perfect mom, daughter, wife, or anything to deserve the same nurturing that you give to others in your life. You are worthy of the investment of time, energy, and focus on your well-being whether you are thriving, failing, or anything in between. And I want every mother struggling with the bullshit idea of balancing it all to know that she deserves to prioritize herself!

I'm not here to make all this sound pretty or easy. I won't be gaslighting you into believing that you can do it all, all the time. I am here to tell you the truth about motherhood and self-care. I won't be using any psychobabble or quoting any research or qualitative data in these pages. I won't tell you to cleanse your crystals, find a quiet corner to meditate, or burn sage in your home (actually that might help a little if you are raising feral demons). And I for damn sure won't be telling you to get up at 4:00 AM, run five miles, or switch your coffee to some rank mushroom alternative. I know you already have more than you can handle on your plate, so I am here to give it to you straight and help you unload that plate like a real mom friend would—because I know you don't have time for any bullshit!

CHAPTER 1:

ACKNOWLEDGE THE LOAD: WTF IS ACTUALLY HAPPENING

I WANTED TO HAVE CHILDREN my entire life, lots of fantastic children. I spent a lot of time daydreaming about how many kids I would have and imagining what they would look like. I fantasized about how many boys and girls there would be and what their little personalities would be like. I would of course breastfeed, make all their food from scratch, and be an attachment, positive-parenting guru. It was going to be the most joyous time of my life because I had the perfect plan for being an ideal mother with exemplary little children.

Nothing could go wrong because I was so prepared. I had a bachelor's in child development and had been working with children since I was a child myself. I worked in summer camps, taught dance classes to every age group, worked in school settings, and babysat. There was nothing more I could have done to be the amazing mom

I conjured up in my head. I just knew I would nail this mom thing [insert maniacal laugh].

Well, as you probably guessed, things haven't exactly gone as planned. When I had my first child, I immediately knew that I was going to have to throw my ideal vision of motherhood out the damn window. I struggled through raw and bloody nipples, postpartum hormonal sweats, and lots of tears to breastfeed my firstborn. It felt like I spent the first six weeks of being a new mom topless, bound to a rocking chair in my room, and crying in pain every time my little bundle of joy latched onto my boob. I was suddenly this zombie of a person who walked around, babbling incoherently, smelling like spit-up, checking that my sleeping baby was still breathing an unreasonable number of times, and wondering just what the hell I got myself into.

I found myself in a silent internal battle trying to reconcile the difference between what I imagined motherhood to be versus the shit show that was happening right before my eyes. Nothing was going as planned, and I was trying to get a grasp on the gamut of conflicting emotions I was feeling: elated and overwhelmed, fulfilled but isolated, and supported yet deceived. And wondering why the hell didn't anyone warn me this was going to happen.

The reality of motherhood versus what I imagined it to be did not match up at all. Little did I know that the weight of motherhood would flip everything upside down, effectively obliterating my life as I knew it. Never did I think that I would have to reimagine who I am. As my family grew, the increasing demands of motherhood shifted my mental, physical, social, emotional, and spiritual needs. With each kid, it took time to adjust to new demands made on me in ways that I had no idea I needed to account for.

I think we all have heard the saying that if you want to make God laugh, tell him your plans. And apparently God saw fit to make my life a comedy of errors. I never had plans to be a mom/stepmom of eight kids. I didn't consider what having a child with a life-threatening medical issue might be like. I definitely didn't think about what could happen if any of these imaginary children were neurodivergent or atypical in any way. I had no idea what it would mean to be the default parent and the toll that can take on a person.

And never did I imagine that my motherhood journey would be filled daily with tears, mental meltdowns, overwhelm, noise aversion, and questioning my sanity. It felt like with the addition of each child, I went through extreme changes that overwhelmed me to the point where I felt like I lost myself. And I didn't even know how far gone I was until I came out on the other end of it and realized how much change I experienced. And I am not going to sit here and act like it is some beautiful process. It's an inevitable, all-consuming process that scrubbed me raw, down to my very soul, leaving me with a completely different version of myself.

The truth is, we have all been force-fed an unattainable version of motherhood, and it's a total scam. We see images of perfect children and mothers who not only have "bounced back" but seem to be thriving. So when you find yourself with a sweaty mom bun, wearing granny panties and a stained bra, and a screaming infant in your arms who won't calm down enough to feed, you think you are doing something wrong. And when you no longer recognize who you are, you must be going insane. But the reality is: This is normal.

You don't expect that becoming a mom means that life as you know it will crumble right before your eyes—and that you are going to have to sort through the remnants to piece back together some version of you. The stability of your daily schedule is snatched away, and it feels like you are being held hostage by the whims of a tiny dictator. You are in a frenzy trying to meet the needs of this demanding little person while struggling to meet your own changing mental, emotional, social, physical, and spiritual needs . . . while running a household. There doesn't seem to be time for you to take a breath and figure anything out. What's more, you're probably struggling with some combination of sleep deprivation, postpartum anxiety, postpartum depression, mom guilt, mom brain, or all of them.

Maybe your children are far past the infant stage, and you are struggling because your kids' schedules have taken over your life and they seem needier than ever. You thought that you would have more balance once they got older, but the reality is it feels like you are running around nonstop and doing everything for everyone but yourself. You are constantly on the go, yet you feel like you can never get anything done on your crazy to-do list. You are drowning and in desperate need of a lifeline, but no one seems to notice. And if one more person says, "I don't know how you do it," you are going to lose your shit!

No matter what stage of motherhood you are in, I am going to guess that you probably picked up this book because you are at the end of your rope. You are overwhelmed, overstimulated, and overtired, and you can't seem to find a way to prioritize yourself in the chaos of motherhood. You are constantly going nonstop, yet you feel as if you never get enough done. And of course, you know you need more time for self-care, but how the hell could you possibly fit that in the mix? And what is self-care even supposed to look like when you barely recognize who you are anymore?

Self-care can be an elusive idea to grasp, especially when you are battling the belief that once you have kids you are no longer a priority. The typical self-care practices pushed on moms are often framed as ways to escape from our lives: bubble baths, girls' trips, spa appointments, or an alcoholic drink at the end of the day. And while days at the spa, weekend getaways, or nightly glasses of wine can be valid forms of self-care, they are either far-fetched, frivolous dreams or small reprieves that don't even begin to address the depth of exhaustion moms are feeling.

In my own journey, I realized that I not only had to change how I practiced self-care but I also had to shift my beliefs about self-care. We have to stop viewing self-care as time to escape from our lives. I am asking you to shift the way you think about self-care to a much longer-term, more strategic point of view. This is not about the momentary relief of an unplanned trip to the nail salon. This is about building habits and practices that consistently address your emotional, mental, physical, social, and spiritual well-being. This is about no longer viewing self-care as a luxury you can't afford or don't have time for but as a necessity you can't function without. I need you to take your self-care as seriously as you take a two-year-old's nap time. . . . It has to happen, or all hell breaks loose!

The other thing I realized was that the act of self-care should not be another thing you try to do perfectly. This is about the practice of caring for yourself consistently over time. One of the key words here is *practice*! That means you are performing an exercise or skill habitually over time in order to improve or maintain proficiency—in your emotional, mental, physical, social, and spiritual well-being. The other key words when discussing self-care are *you*, *your*, and *yourself* because the practice has to work for *you*, in *your* life, so you can maintain *your*self.

With all that said, the first step in the process is to get real about what your day-to-day life actually looks like in order to give yourself a more realistic understanding of the who, what, when, where, and how of all the shit that is on your plate. You need to get a clear picture of your current reality so that you know what you are actually doing within the twenty-four hours you get day in and day out. I would venture to say that so many of you don't fully count all that you do in a day. The number of times I have heard a mom say she didn't get anything done today when she probably did three times more than the average person tells me that a lot of moms discount so many of the things they manage on a daily basis.

Many of us are in auto mode. We do without even realizing how much we are doing: the physical day-to-day work, the planning, the emotional regulation, the mental load, and more. All too often, the importance of what you do is overlooked, oversimplified, and underappreciated. And you are probably just as guilty of undermining the load you carry whether it's because of denial, being too overwhelmed to realize, or being conditioned to believe that no matter what you do, it's never enough. But this shit has to stop. You do so much for your family, and I need you to take the time to recognize that!

How many hours do you spend breastfeeding or changing diapers? How much time do you spend playing the role of Uber mom? How much homework do you do with your kids? How many snacks and meals do you make a day? How many hours do you work? How long do you spend doing chores around the house? How much time do you spend grocery shopping? How often do you restock household items like toilet paper or cleaning supplies? How many activities are your kids involved in, and how much of your time does that take? How much sleep are you really getting at night? How many schedules are you maintaining? How much time in your day do you spend holding a child, wiping tears, putting Band-Aids on nonexistent booboos, saying the same doggone thing over and over, responding to "Mom!" 5,378 times, breaking up ridiculous fights, redirecting behavior, reminding kids to just brush their dang teeth . . . ?

This may seem daunting, but I am going to walk you through documenting all that you do in your day-to-day life. Please do not use this process to judge yourself. That's not what this is about. This is about documenting all the labor that you may or may not consider. You are just taking stock of your time so that you can make the invisible load visible. This is to give you a clearer picture of all the things you take care of so that you have a more accurate picture of how you spend your time.

Make a List of the Motherload

So, let's get started on this long, exhausting, overwhelming "motherload" list. It may seem mind-boggling, but it is quite cathartic when all is said and done. Seeing all that you do gives you perspective and begins to alleviate the mom guilt that is often the driving force for Super Mom Syndrome (we'll talk about that later). It also helps you see all the things that are taking up your mental, physical, emotional, social, or spiritual capacity that may or may not be of importance to you. I am not going to lie: This process is going to take an investment of your time, but I promise that spending time to acknowledge all that you do is worth its weight in gold.

How do you do this? Let's break this down into steps so it is a little easier. This process is to simply take stock of your motherload and put it into a tangible list. I don't care if you think it's an insignificant task. Write it down! I don't care if you don't even do the task yourself. If you manage the tasks—like your kids doing chores, for instance—write it down! If it's just something you think about, write it down! If it's something you constantly have to remind your kids to do, write it down! Fielding all the autobot calls from your kids' schools, write it down! Write down every damn app you check for school and sports activities for after-school programs. Write it all down!

You can write it by hand in a notebook or on scratch paper. You can do it on the go in your notes app on your phone or type it all in a Word doc. You can jot it down in the note pages in the back of your planner. You can even build an entire color-coded Excel file if that's what works for you. It doesn't matter how you record it because this taking stock of every bit of mental, physical, emotional, social, or spiritual labor you undertake is just for your eyes. If you feel shame, guilt, or judgment bubbling up, that's okay. Take a moment to acknowledge the feeling and then let it go. But I have a hunch you'll actually experience the opposite.

Step 1

The first question you need to address is "*What care tasks do you do on a daily basis*?"

Take seven separate sheets of paper or create seven sections and label them with the days of the week.

Take seven minutes per day to write down care tasks that you do for all those who fall under your care for every day of the week.

These are typically tasks, chores, and errands that tend to recur on a daily basis and are never-ending. Write down everything you can think of: getting everyone up in the morning, making lunches, making breakfast, driving to school, checking backpacks, signing school papers, checking school and sports apps, dishes, laundry, appointment making, meal planning, grocery shopping, cooking, diaper changing, breastfeeding, taxiing to extracurricular activities, planning weekends, organizing playdates, volunteering at school, picking up messes, wiping down sticky surfaces, and anything else that comes up for you.

Don't qualify it, just write it.

There is no right or wrong way to go about this. It may work for you to go through the timeline of your day and write down tasks according to your daily schedule. Maybe it works better to group tasks by category, such as school, household management, and so on. You may get stuck and have to spend a few minutes thinking. That's okay. The important thing is that you start writing and keep logging everything that comes to mind.

Step 2

For one week, carry your list with you and add anything that comes up throughout the day that you may have missed. It may be making multiple meals for dinner, looking for matching shoes, or running to the grocery store for the third time in a week.

If you have a repetitive daily task such as breastfeeding, changing diapers, wiping butts, or giving medication, create a tally section so that you know how many times a day you are doing it (such as, Breastfeeding: III).

Step 2 can happen simultaneously with the remaining steps. For Steps 3 to 7, you will need to block off seventy minutes of uninterrupted time.

Step 3

The second question is "*What household management tasks are you responsible for?*"

For ten minutes, write down any tasks that you are in charge of doing or managing pertaining to your household. This can include anything from keeping the kitchen and pantry stocked, cleaning, bills you are in charge of paying, managing the kids' chores, and so on. If you have to think about it, that means you are doing mental labor to get it done. Write it down!

Take a five-minute break.

Step 4

The third question is "*What tasks do you perform on a weekly, monthly, or annual basis*?"

For ten minutes, write down any tasks that don't take place on a daily basis, such as doctors' appointments, summer camp registration, holiday planning, family vacation, birthday parties, and so on.

Take a five-minute break.

Step 5

The fourth question is "*What tasks do you take on that have to do with your parenting partner*?" (Answer this question whether you are in a romantic relationship or not.)

Take ten minutes to write down any tasks that include planning for or with your parenting partner, from scheduling date nights or having sex to family planning time. If you are not romantically involved with your parenting partner, this may include planning visitation, communicating about the kids, or managing transitions between homes. And if you don't have an active parenting partner (regardless of whether they live in the home or not), think about the mental, physical, emotional, and spiritual work you do to compensate. Some examples may be having to cover for their lack of involvement (i.e., make up reasons they didn't show up that won't break your kiddo's heart), managing all the finances on your own, managing your kids' expectations and emotions, etc.

Take a five-minute break. Hell, you might need longer for this step in particular, depending on how pissed off you are. And that's okay because you deserve to be pissed.

Step 6

At this point, I want you to take a moment and look over your list. The fifth question is "*Are you on the list*?"

I am going to guess that you have probably overlooked a lot of things you have to do that are not for anyone but you. So now, think about all the tasks you must complete for yourself and take ten minutes to put yourself on the list.

This might include tasks like tracking your period, work tasks, personal doctor appointments, getting gas, hair appointments, keeping up with text messages, and so on and so forth. You don't need to get as specific as, say, putting in your contacts daily, but write a general list of things you do for yourself.

Take a five-minute break.

Step 7

The sixth question is "*What activities do you participate in that take up more of your time than you care to admit*?"

For ten minutes, I need you to ask yourself: Are you scrolling social media for hours a day? Do you like to watch trash reality TV at the end of the night for longer than you planned? Do you get stuck playing Candy Crush, Solitaire, Merge Mansion, or any other game for more time than you would like to admit?

It's okay. We all do it. And again this is not a place for judgment, just acknowledgment. So write it down! And I will openly acknowledge that, according to my phone, I easily spend an hour-plus a day playing one or more of the aforementioned games.

Step 8

Sit with your list for a few days. Keep it accessible, and anytime something comes up that you didn't previously think of, write it down—all the things that never really quite get done but are constantly on your mind and all the little tasks that you do day in and day out that go unnoticed. You will be surprised by the things that you overlook because you do them without even thinking. It may be picking up after everyone at night or remembering everyone's medication schedules. No matter how minor it seems or how long it's been on your to-do list, write it down!

Acknowledge the Invisible Labor

Why am I putting so much emphasis on telling you to write it all down? I know this is a tedious and maybe even overwhelming task, but it is really important for you to see everything that you do, right in front of your face, all at once. When I did this for myself, I realized that I didn't give myself credit for so much of what I did every single day. I often didn't account for the small, mundane things that tend to occupy my day—things like sorting through school papers, checking the thirty-seven apps my kids need for school, making appointments, answering text and e-mails, negotiating bedtime, redirecting fighting kids, and planning, shopping for, and making meal after meal.

These are the inevitable things that happen every day that we tend to overlook as insignificant. But the truth is that these mundane things are the everyday tasks that make up the invisible labor that constantly takes up your emotional, mental, physical, social, and spiritual capacity. Not acknowledging them continues to keep the load invisible not only to others but to yourself. Your list substantiates all that you do and validates why you are feeling stressed out, overwhelmed, overstimulated, anxious, exhausted, or any combination of feelings.

Now, read your list again with that new perspective and take a deep breath because—*whew, girl*—that's a lot! I need you to acknowledge the fact that it took over a week to get a comprehensive list of all the things you do. Being faced with the list you created may bring up big feelings for you, and it's okay to sit with those feelings, but most of all, be proud of yourself for finally acknowledging all that you do. Good job, Momma!

CHAPTER 2:

COME TO TERMS WITH YOUR REALITY: You Can't Do All This Shit!

IF YOU DIDN'T ALREADY KNOW, it should now be abundantly clear how much crap you are thinking about, worrying about, planning, managing, and doing in what feels like a never-ending cycle. And as a woman and a caretaker, you have probably been conditioned to believe that in order to be perceived as a good mother/partner/wife/daughter/friend/career woman, you are *required* to do all these things, all the time. So you run around in perpetual circles trying to be good at everything and beating yourself up for all the things for which you deem yourself a failure.

But the thing is, modern-day motherhood is asking entirely too much of us, and I believe we have all collectively hit the wall of our limitations. Moms have to start openly admitting that we have these limitations—not only to other people, but also to ourselves—and drop the facade of perfection that is chipping away at our well-being.

There are things you know you do well, and some things you know you aren't good at or don't like to do. When you don't feel like you are good at something, that often leads to avoidance, followed by mom guilt, followed by beating yourself up for not being good at the thing you are not good at. We need to get more comfortable with admitting where we struggle. It is okay to admit if you are bad at cooking, or you never wanted to breastfeed, or you hate cleaning, or you are not the kind of mom to get on the floor and play cars or dolls, or you can't help your kid with math, or you struggle with patience every single day.

On the other hand, there are things you are damn good at that you probably don't acknowledge to yourself, but you deserve credit when you are good at something. If you throw amazing themed birthday parties for your kiddos, own it. If you are the master of co-ordinating multiple schedules, be proud of that. And if your family devours your meals without complaint because you are a great cook, relish those moments.

I can't tell you how many times I have admitted a perceived shortcoming to another mom only to find out she is struggling with the same damn thing. The very first mom friend I made was by sharing all the gory parts of my birth story right down to the fact that I pooped on the delivery table. Did she judge me? No, because the very same happened to her and now she is one of my dearest friends, whom I trust with my deepest, darkest secrets. I have admitted to experiencing panic attacks to a fellow dance mom, divulged marriage problems to a friend who was experiencing the same thing, listed perimenopause symptoms with another soccer mom on the sidelines of a game, and so many other things. And not once has another mother made me feel judged or less than.

I would even go so far as to say that allowing myself to be vulnerable in that way has helped me to connect with other moms on a much deeper level. So, I am just going to admit—right here, right now—to some of the things I think I regularly fail at as a mom.

I yell at my kids more often than I would like to admit. I also struggle to follow through with discipline, promises, and so much more when it comes to my kids because I just can't keep up with all the things I am supposed to remember. I battle time blindness and always think I can do more than I actually can in the time that I have. And I think I am overly critical with my kids, especially my daughter, and even though I know it stems from my own anxiety or insecurities, I have trouble stopping.

I admit that I tend to verbally express myself when I am struggling with or processing something, so this may be easier for me than other moms. But I feel like the more I share, the less afraid I am of being judged. As a matter of fact, I went viral for telling the truth about my version of motherhood. When my daughter was about eleven months old, I posted a picture on social media of me breastfeeding my daughter while sitting on the toilet with my bathroom in total disarray. I shared this picture with my measly 400 followers because I felt that it so perfectly captured the phase of motherhood I was in, and I was sure one of my mom friends would relate to it. The next thing I knew, the picture was trending on Reddit, and I had interview requests coming in from all over the world.

I got the opportunity to respond to all the hoopla about my breastfeeding picture with an article in the *Huffington Post* where I admitted to some of my failures and bad habits. But I also shared that in spite of all my perceived faults, I still felt that I was a good mother. And it was so cathartic to give the middle finger to the expectations hurled at me and be honest about where I fell short and what I was damn good at. Of course, the trolls came out of the woodwork, and I was called everything from a terrible mom to a nasty cow. But what mattered to me more was the number of moms who thanked me for sharing my truth in motherhood:

> "I'm so proud that anyone can post such realness. It takes courage, it shouldn't, because it's reality."
>
> "Motherhood isn't all snuggles and smiles. . . . It is messy and chaotic and occasionally embarrassing."
>
> "This is real. We 'like' photos every day on here that are pretty photos but of fake life. Props to you for sharing all aspects of what real life looks like!"
>
> "I love seeing moms in those very real moments that make me realize that we have no reason to be ashamed of those everyday tasks no one else sees! Phone, toilet, nursing baby, and cabinet contents on the floor. So many years of mornings for myself and millions of other moms!!!"
>
> "I'm a new mom and I did it once, because my tummy was upset and my baby was screaming for me. I couldn't let my month-old baby wait. I felt terrible and guilty after. Later I told my mom, and she just laughed. She said I wouldn't believe how many times she did that with us kids! It's great to see moms coming together and sharing the truth about it, so when things that aren't so pretty happen, you know! Thank you for sharing."

I have been asked if I regret posting such a private moment on the Internet. Even though it got way more attention than I ever fathomed possible, I would post it 1,000 times over again and again. The experience showed me that most moms just want to feel less alone as we navigate our day-to-day life and be seen and appreciated for the mundane, invisible work we do.

As moms, we tend to be the hardest on ourselves. We often beat ourselves up for circumstances that we can't change, we shy away from compliments that we deserve, and we shun opportunities for support or growth because we think we are supposed to be able to handle everything on our own. But what if you changed the narrative? What would happen if you shifted your perspective to celebrating your strengths, accepting your weaknesses, taking advantage of opportunities, and confronting barriers?

SWOB

Let's start to shift your narrative by taking a SWOB of your life. In other words, let's take some time to identify **Strengths**, evaluate **Weaknesses**, recognize **Opportunities**, and acknowledge **Barriers**. Don't panic! This is simply a framework for assessing where you thrive, where you struggle, what is getting in your way, and what opportunities are available to you. It's an exercise that can help you get a big-picture idea of your reality so that you can take steps to focus on the positive and minimize the negative.

Prior to becoming a mom, I worked as a certified strategic planner and helped developed plans for arts education in local school districts. I always started the planning process with a tool called SWOT analysis. In its simplest form, it helps organizations identify their internal strengths (assets and capabilities) and weaknesses (areas for improvement or support). And the analysis examines external opportunities and potentially challenging threats. It didn't take me long to realize that, as the primary caregiver in my home, I was basically running a small business, and I wondered if I could apply this technique to my home life. I gave it a try, and with a few adjustments, the SWOT analysis became a SWOB analysis.

So how do you do a SWOB analysis? Start with a blank sheet of paper and divide it into four quadrants. Label across the top *Supportive* and *Disruptive* and along the side two quadrants *Intrinsic* and *Extrinsic*. Then label the top two quadrants *Strengths* and *Weaknesses*, and the bottom two quadrants *Opportunities* and *Barriers*.

	Supportive	**Disruptive**
Intrinsic	Strengths	Weaknesses
Extrinsic	Opportunities	Barriers

Before you start, let's break a few things down so that you have some guidance on how to approach this:

Intrinsic means the qualities you naturally embody, whether they are supportive or disruptive of your goals: your attitude, beliefs, abilities, proclivities, predispositions, tendencies, disabilities, health.

Extrinsic means the external factors that affect you: financial status, marital status, job, family structure, trainings, degrees, where you reside.

Supportive are things that are favorable to your goals, setting you up for success.

Disruptive are things that are distracting, obtrusions to your goals, or work in opposition to how you want things to go.

I need you to understand that a crucial part of this process is that you be brutally honest with yourself. Nobody has to see this but you, so drop your self-judgment and face your reality. In order to properly address your needs, you have to have a clear and accurate picture of them. Acknowledge the good, the bad, the easy, and the challenging—not only acknowledge it, but own it!

Strengths

Write down the intrinsic qualities you have that support you in being the best version of yourself. When you are asking yourself these questions, look for patterns in your behavior or thinking.

- What practices, mindset, or knowledge are you already using?
- What is working well for you?
- What do you enjoy doing?
- What about your parenting makes you especially proud?
- What makes you unique from other parents?
- What are your internal resources? What natural abilities do you have? What skills do you possess that support you in

your parenting (e.g., patience, cooking skills, perspectives, or attitudes)?

- What does your spouse or parenting partner think you are good at?
- What positive qualities do you have?
- What do other people admire about you?

Again, let's keep it simple. You don't need a fancy sentence structure or anything. This is just about getting your ideas on paper. Some examples you may list in this category are as follows:

- Great cook
- Love to clean
- Great at playing with kids
- Great communicator
- I am healthy and active
- Love taking my kids on adventures
- I forgive easily
- I go with the flow
- I am easygoing
- I am a planner
- I am resourceful
- Supportive of my kids' interest
- Calm in a crisis
- Adaptable
- Confident
- Intuitive
- A fierce, strong advocate for my child
- Open-minded
- Can let things go
- Resilient
- Accountable
- Self-aware

Don't be afraid to ask people in your life how they might answer these questions. They can offer a perspective you don't have, and their answers may surprise you.

Weaknesses

Write down personal habits or internal issues that can get in the way of you being the best version of yourself. Again, look for any patterns in your behavior or thinking that could be matters of concern.

- Are you experiencing a lack of motivation or finding it hard to make time in your day?
- What is not working well for you?
- Where do you struggle the most?
- What do you wish you were better at?
- What makes you feel bad as a parent?
- What is something you do that makes it challenging for you to achieve your goals?
- What do your kids complain about the most when it comes to your way of parenting? (The answers may be hard to hear, but there is helpful information in them. They may say you are on the phone too much, you yell too much, or you never listen to them. Your immediate reaction may be defensive, but try to hear them out with an open mind.)
- In what areas does your spouse or parenting partner think you need support?

Here are some examples of weaknesses. And what I may consider a weakness, you may consider a strength, so go with what feels right to you.

- Impatient
- Yell

- Noise aversion
- Hold grudges
- Inconsistent
- Have trouble regulating emotions
- Feel constantly exhausted
- Micromanage my kids
- Lose my temper easily
- No structure or routine at home
- Lack of self-care
- Tend to be critical
- Feel overworked and underappreciated
- Self-critical
- Tend to take on too much
- Forgetful
- Unmotivated
- Perfectionist
- Procrastinator
- Poor mental health
- Struggle with implementing coping strategies
- I hate cooking
- I hate cleaning
- Easily overwhelmed

Opportunities

Write down what or who you have in place to support you in achieving your goals. These are external supports that you can regularly count on.

- What structures, systems, or resources are you currently using?

- What support do you already have in place?
- Who outside of yourself can regularly care for your children?
- What external resources are at your disposal—such as after-school care, therapist, grocery delivery service, housekeeping services, meal delivery, and so on—that help you as a parent?
- What technology helps you out? Social media groups, calendar apps, crockpot/Instapot (yes, a crockpot counts as technology that supports you in these mom streets! You can try to fight me on that one, but I will go to my grave over that argument).
- What do you have access to that you may not be using to your advantage, such as free tutoring services or people who are willing to help, but you don't know what to ask of them.

Some examples may include

- Free aftercare at school
- Online support group
- Health insurance coverage
- Insurance that covers mental health services
- Amazon membership and subscription services
- Children are old enough to contribute to household chores
- Family is supportive and lives nearby
- Support services provided by school for children with additional needs through IEPs or 504s
- Delivery services for food, laundry, and goods
- Paid services such as cleaning or tutoring
- Helplines to call for support and resources
- Internet access
- Mother's helper
- In-person parenting groups

- Social organizations for moms
- Nanny or babysitter
- Grocery pickup services
- Welfare
- Access to food stamps
- Coupons
- Supportive and active spouse or partner
- Supportive friends
- Instapot

Barriers

Write down who or what prevents you from achieving your goals. Barriers should be considered external things or situations that cannot be resolved without external support.

- Do you face financial challenges?
- Do you have an overwhelming amount of commitments?
- What often stands in the way of achieving your self-care goals?
- What commitments, responsibilities, or relationships stand in your way?
- What obstacles are you currently facing?
- Are you currently in a healthy and safe living situation?

Some examples of barriers are

- Limited finances
- No insurance
- No friends
- My children have special needs
- Lack of spouse or partner support
- Lack of social interaction
- Depression

- Anxiety
- Unemployed
- No childcare
- Job severely limits time to parent or care for myself due to travel or hour requirements
- No Internet access
- No washer/dryer at home
- Lack of transportation
- Unsafe home environment
- Limited access to services or resources
- Lack of skills in needed areas

This Is *Your* Journey

I want to emphasize that this exercise is not about dwelling on what you have or don't have or what you can and cannot do. This is about recognizing your strengths and opportunities so that you can lean into them and identifying your weaknesses and barriers so that you can bring in support and build capacity in those areas. It's also about taking stock of what practices, mindsets, tools, resources, and people you have in place and the challenges and barriers that may be getting in your way before you begin to build your self-care practice. First, become aware of what you are dealing with so that you can then make changes to move you forward effectively in your journey to a better you.

Now that you have made a SWOB analysis of your life, let's take a moment to reflect on what came up for you during the process. These questions don't have right or wrong answers. This is more about identifying the information you may have learned about yourself during this exercise.

What did you notice about how you were feeling during this process?

____

____

____

____

____

____

____

Example: At first I felt stuck when thinking about what my strengths were, and I realized I tend to focus on what I do wrong. I also noticed that I tend to overlook a lot of things that are opportunities because I thought they were too small to matter, but I saw that small things add up. Listing barriers brought up a lot of negative feelings for me.

What came up that inspires or excites you? What came up that concerns you?

____

____

____

____

____

____

____

Example: When I asked my family what I am good at as a mom, it inspired me because they saw things in me that I don't necessarily see in myself. I also got excited because I realized that I have a lot of things working in my favor that can help me take steps toward a better self-care practice. I am concerned that I allow the bigger barriers to overwhelm me because that is what has happened in the past. And my tendency to get overwhelmed and shut down is a big worry of mine.

What new perspective (positive or negative) did you gain about yourself through this SWOB analysis?

____

____

____

____

____

____

____

Example: I focus on what I do wrong or what isn't working way more than I care to admit. I guess I knew that before, but struggling with filling out the strengths and opportunities section really brought that to light for me.

What strengths and opportunities will you use to better support you in your self-care practice?

____

____

____

____

____

____

____

Example: My tendency to get overwhelmed and shut down greatly affects my self-care, and I can probably use some support in that area through therapy. The stress my job causes has become a significant barrier to my self-care, and I may need to consider having a conversation with my boss about changes we can make or maybe even finding a new job.

My hope is that you begin to see this as an empowering, liberating process that gives you some insight into where you are doing great, where you could use some help, opportunities you should take advantage of, and barriers you need help breaking. Most importantly, you need to come to understand this is *your* journey. Your best friend, your mom, your sister, your neighbor, your kid's teacher, or your fav content creator doesn't live the same life, is not raising the same kids, comes from a different background, doesn't have the same challenges, doesn't have your unique talents, and doesn't share the same life experiences or perspectives. That doesn't mean you are better or less than anyone else. It just means you are on a journey that is uniquely yours.

CHAPTER 3:

RECLAIM YOUR SELF-CARE:
This Is Your Fucking Rodeo

WHEN I FIRST BECAME A MOM, I failed to recognize that motherhood is such a personal journey. It won't look anything like anyone else's journey, and more importantly, it definitely will not look like the imaginary version of motherhood that exists before kids are even in the picture. It took me quite some time to come to terms with the fact that I had to stop comparing myself to others or to who I thought I would be.

I never imagined what it would be like to be a stepmom. I didn't once think about the care for a kid with a life-threatening medical condition. I never daydreamed about what kind of mom I would be if I had a kid with special needs. I had no plans for adoption. I didn't make any plans for how I would handle being a touched-out mom with a noise aversion trying to get four tired, overly hyper kids to bed night after night without screaming at everybody, "Go the *fuck* to *BED*!" And I couldn't have begun to imagine all the things that come along with being the primary/default parent with a parenting partner who often has to work out of town.

It took me one too many bouts with my mental health to realize it is up to me to decide what kind of mother I want or need to be and how I can best meet the needs of my family. This also applies to my self-care. My self-care practices have to be for me! I deserve to build a practice that serves my needs for whatever my stage of life is. And my self-care practices will need to shift as I grow and change as a mother, an individual, a romantic partner, and so on. What worked for me as a young mom of a toddler doesn't necessarily serve me as an over-forty, perimenopausal mom of four kids.

The minute you log onto social media, you get bombarded with all the self-care routines: the perfect morning routine with meditation and matcha lattes at 5:00 AM; the calming nighttime routine with a twenty-five-step skin-care routine; the easy workout routine with the perfect combination of strength, cardiovascular, and flexibility training that takes the equivalent time of a part-time job. Meanwhile, your mornings are an exercise in survival of the fittest and you think matcha lattes taste like boiled grass, you are lucky if you manage to wash your makeup off at night before you face-plant into your pillow, and the only exercise you have done recently is running after feral children who insist on attempting to destroy themselves two or three times a day. These Instagrammable self-care routines seem like unreachable goals for you right now, and you are probably right. You aren't going to go overnight from dragging yourself through the day to suddenly doing all the self-care things. That's a shortcut to complete burnout.

We so often feel the pressure to "mom boss" to the tenth degree so that we can be everything to everyone in our homes, be productive every minute of the day both at home and at work, and make it all look effortless. We feel guilty for not being more efficient with our time so we can fit more things in, we turn hobbies into side hustles, and we have turned multitasking into a master skill. Meanwhile, we are burying our misery and anxiety in busyness, and we can't figure out why we are so tired.

It's overwhelming—and that often leads to self-care being pushed to the bottom of the to-do list right along with all the other things that most likely won't get done. But you know you can't continue to sideline your self-care and run yourself into the ground. So you are probably asking yourself, How do I do this? How do I start prioritizing my needs without feeling overburdened with yet another thing to do? How do I even begin to figure out what I need or want to do for myself? How will I have the time for any of this? What could I possibly squeeze into my schedule?

Since having kids, have you taken the time to intentionally think about what self-care looks like for you? It's really quite normal if you haven't, and you are definitely not alone. Most of us don't consider self-care because as soon as you add a child to your life, you have been programmed to believe that everything you do should rotate around the needs of said kiddo. So you try to power through sleep deprivation, postpartum depression, postpartum anxiety, stress, overwhelm, and lack of support—and balancing it all because you were made to believe that's how it works.

I powered my way through motherhood, thinking that the most important thing I could do was put myself on the back burner and prioritize being a mother and a wife. I literally sobbed, sweated, and bled through the first six weeks of breastfeeding my firstborn child before finding out he had tongue tie and a congenital heart defect. Then I mustered my way through the diagnosis of the congenital heart defect, shoving all my fears and anxiety down so that I could focus on my kid's health. Once he had open heart surgery, I focused on literally and figuratively nursing him back to health.

I was so relieved to be done with the whirlwind of constantly visiting our pediatrician, cardiologist, and nutritionist that I figured it was time for a second child. Not even a year after she was born, we experienced a family emergency that called for the adoption of our third child; subsequently, I started having panic attacks. But I convinced myself that it was no big deal and that I was fine. I soldiered on, and we moved to a new house while I was pregnant with kiddo number four. At just four months postpartum, my husband had to work out of the country for six weeks, my mother-in-law passed away, one of my stepkids ended up in the hospital in need of a blood transfusion—and I was days away from having a complete meltdown.

The point is, once I became a mother, I always had a reason to push away my own needs. I kept telling myself I would focus on me after the heart surgery, after I had my second baby, after my adoptive kiddo settled in, after . . . after . . . after. There was always a reason someone else was more important than my needs until I mentally collapsed and fell into a dark hole where I never want to return.

Don't get me wrong. I wasn't necessarily miserable. There were many happy moments, and I was so damn good at masking my struggles that I didn't even recognize how much I was struggling. And to be honest, there are so many black holes in my memories because, looking back, I spent so much time in survival mode, stuffing my feelings and ignoring my needs. All the alarms were going off in my body, and I could practically feel the cortisol pumping through my veins. But I just kept pushing through because how could I possibly think about myself when everyone around me needed me so much?

Does any of this sound familiar? I share all of this with you to help you understand I know firsthand that starting on a journey of self-care can seem dauntingly impossible. But if you don't start at least thinking about what self-care can look like for you, you will eventually get to the point where your mind and body will shut down on you, and you will be forced to learn how to practice a radical level of self-care.

Five Areas of Self-Care

So where do you start? The goal is to create a well-rounded self-care practice that addresses all areas of your life. This part of the process is designed to ensure that you have addressed the five major areas of self-care: emotional, mental, physical, social, and spiritual. That doesn't mean that you need to tend to all areas all the time. That's impossible. But being intentional about addressing all facets of self-care will help you implement what you need in order to reach an overall better state of well-being.

Emotional

Your emotional health encompasses the ability to identify, feel, acknowledge, and constructively act on negative and positive emotions. Instead of stuffing your feelings and barreling through, you have to find ways to honor your emotions and process them in a healthy way.

Ways to practice emotional self-care:

- Practice positive self-talk.
- Openly express both positive and negative feelings.
- Prioritize sleep.
- Share your feelings with someone you trust.
- Take intentional deep breaths.

Mental

Your mental health encompasses your ability to cope with the normal stresses of life and demonstrate a level of resilience. Whether you are a stay-at-home mom, work-at-home mom, or working mom, you should feel productive and fruitful in some aspects of your life and know that it is okay to feel like a hot mess in other aspects of your life. This also encompasses acknowledging and actively treating mental illness or a mental health crisis. The key is having strategies to cope with the ups and downs of life.

Ways to practice mental self-care:

- Identify mental health challenges and seek support.
- Join a virtual or in-person support group.
- Attend therapy.
- Set healthy boundaries.
- Say "no."

Physical

Your physical health encompasses the health of your body, nutrition, exercise, physical touch, and, yes, your sexual needs. As much as moms are portrayed as being superhuman, you are still a physical being with physical needs that require attention. This includes drinking water, practicing a regular workout routine, visiting your doctor, eating balanced meals, sleeping, and having sex (even if it's with yourself).

Ways to practice physical self-care:

- Take daily walks.
- Work out on a regular basis.
- Take stretching breaks throughout your day.
- Add more vegetables to your diet.
- Keep up-to-date with annual appointments like Pap smears, breast exams, dental cleanings, and eye checkups.

Social

Your social health encompasses your relationships and social interactions. Humans are naturally social people, and you need social interaction outside of your kids. Whether you are an introvert, extrovert, or some mixture of both, communing with others and maintaining healthy relationships are a needed part of self-care. This includes making and maintaining friends, going out, interacting in various social situations, and social time that doesn't revolve around your children.

Ways to practice social self-care:

- Engage in online communities.
- Spend time with friends and family.
- Stay connected with loved ones.
- Plan face-to-face time with friends and family.
- Start a conversation with someone new . . . a mom at your kid's soccer practice, the neighbor you keep running into, or that coworker who seems kind of cool.

Spiritual

Your spiritual health encompasses the practices that reflect your values, bring you hope, purpose, and peace, and give you a broader perspective. This area of self-care is deeply personal and not necessarily connected to a religious practice. You have to find what works for you.

Ways to practice spiritual self-care:

- Meditate or pray.
- Attend a place of worship.
- Participate in spiritual practices.
- Self-reflect through journaling.
- Practice gratitude.

Envisioning Your Self-Care Practice

Here is where I push you to start imagining the ways you could better care for yourself beyond the haphazard self-care "practices" that currently pepper your life. In what ways can you better support your needs? Is there something you need to do for yourself that you are dreading but you know will lead to less stress? What small things can you do for yourself every day to help you get through the hard times? What are some of the things you wished you did for yourself? Have you imagined what a well-rested, supported, and cared-for you looks and feels like?

These may be hard questions for you because I am pretty sure nobody has really asked you what you want for yourself for quite some time. You are probably not even used to asking yourself these questions. It may bring up feelings like anger, sadness, anxiety, or even regret. Girl, it's understandable to be triggered by these questions. Take a deep breath and allow yourself to feel all the feelings that come up! And every time another feeling comes up that makes you want to throw in the towel, take three intentional deep breaths and then keep going. This is a journey that will take time and some patience, but I am asking you to trust the process.

Step 1

The very first step I want you to take is to write down the things you are already doing to practice self-care. Once you start writing things down, my guess is that you are practicing more than you give yourself credit for. Now hold on . . . before you start tearing yourself down because you think you aren't doing anything for yourself, start with very basic care tasks. I don't care what anybody says, I will argue till my dying breath that basic tasks like showering, eating, washing your face, sleeping, and drinking water all count because they are the fundamental building blocks for any self-care routine.

Next, think through your days and weeks and jot down the things you regularly do for yourself. Do you take walks, have a workout routine, or eat healthy meals? Do you make a habit of chatting with your friends or family on the phone? Do you get your hair or nails done? Do you listen to a podcast, book, or your favorite music in the car, at home, or in the office? Are you enjoying sex with yourself or someone else? Do you sit in your car for fifteen minutes after driving home from work?

Go back and review the strengths and opportunities you listed in the SWOB analysis that you already have. Do you have a practice of meditation that helps you calm down? Do you regularly spend time with supportive girlfriends? Do you use paid services such as a nanny, babysitter, or cleaning services? Do you meal plan? Do you have a parenting partner who shares the load? Do you stay up-to-date on your doctor visits?

These are all forms of self-care, so write them down. And be sure to draw a line under the list so that you separate the things that you already do from the next lists you are going to make.

Step 2

This is where I want you to dream about all possibilities of self-care. Take ten minutes to write down any self-care ideas that come to mind without limiting or judging yourself.

Write down any form of self-care you can think of. It doesn't have to make sense or be appealing to anyone but you. You can start with something as simple as going to the bathroom without an audience or eating an uninterrupted meal sitting down (okay . . . so, maybe those two things aren't so simple, but you get my drift). Or it can be as big as taking an annual trip with your husband, a group of girlfriends, or by your damn self. Think small and think big.

Actually, I want you to think about this as if you are building yourself an unlimited buffet of self-care options. I'm talking about a Vegas-style buffet where the options range the whole gamut. And don't worry about perfection, or what's possible and what's not. Just write down whatever comes to you. You can write a single word like "rested" or a simple phrase like "get healthy." It could be a full sentence like "I want a clean house but get somebody else to do it." If you find yourself really stuck, refer to the appendix for self-care ideas.

Step 3

Self-care is not always about all the fun, restful, or luxurious things you want to do for yourself. Sometimes taking better care of yourself is about doing the things that you do not want to do, that thing you have been avoiding at all cost, the elephant in the room that is making it hard for you to breathe. Take ten minutes to write down self-care practices that you actively avoid.

This is where I also want you to refer back to your weaknesses and barriers you listed in your SWOB exercise. Think about the things you are struggling with and what self-care actions you can take to combat them.

You may really need to start therapy because you are dealing with a past trauma or mental health crisis that can't be addressed with a hot cup of tea. If you have crippling financial debt, then creating a budget, cutting expenses, or finding new sources of income may be where you need to start. And if you are in a relationship that is unhealthy, abusive, or draining you mentally and emotionally, it may be time for you to leave that mofo: That is, you may want to start the process of breaking up, moving out, or getting that divorce.

Please know the fight that you are fighting is self-care. So instead of allowing that negative voice in your head to berate you for being in the position you are in, take ownership of the fact that you are doing the hard work to change things. Whatever you want to do to make those changes, write it down and give yourself the credit you deserve.

Step 4

Use the following questions to prompt you and get the ideas flowing on a deeper level. Take another ten minutes to list any ideas you get from the questions below:

- **What do you want for you?** We all have things that we want for ourselves whether we voice them aloud or not. You are constantly thinking about everyone else, and it's time to start thinking about what you want. You may want more quiet time, more support from your family, or designated time to yourself.
- **How do you want to feel?** Sometimes it is hard to nail down what you want to do, but you may be able to communicate how you want to feel. Writing down things like strong,

healthy, or healed are valid ways to start to get ideas down on paper.

- **What do you want to look like?** Some may say it's vain, but how you look on the outside so often affects how you feel on the inside. So don't be hesitant to write down things like look better in clothes, get a better wardrobe, improve your skin.
- **What goals do you want to accomplish?** When you spend the majority of your time doing everything for everyone but yourself, you overlook setting personal goals for yourself. It may seem selfish, but pursuing your goals is a very important form of self-care. Maybe you want to go back to school, write a book, or build your financial nest egg.
- **What do you want your day-to-day schedule to include?** Self-care is something that you should be thinking about as a daily part of your life. Doing things like taking a walk, journaling, reading, or moving your body on a daily basis is entirely possible.
- **What is something fun you want to do?** In the midst of all this adulting, we so often forget to have a little fun. Life can't always be about bills, work, and caring for others. Every once in a while, you can make time for some fun in your life. Think about a night out with your girlfriends, going to a flea market or cozy bookstore, or attending a concert by your favorite musician.
- **Is there anything new you want to learn?** Just because you are an adult doesn't mean you can't enjoy learning a new skill. Take a singing class, learn a new language, sign up for a dance class, or try your hand at crafting.
- **Who do you want as a part of your support system?** Having

a support system is a big factor in supporting your self-care practice. Think about who you wished was a bigger part of your life or people you would like to add to your life like new friends or maybe even a supportive romantic partner.

- **What rejuvenates you?** When we think of self-care, we tend to think of the things that provide us with stress relief. But most of us don't often think about the things that "fill our cup," that is, the things that rejuvenate our spirit and infuse us with energy. For you that may be attending church, spending quality time with a friend, or starting your day with yoga.
- **What are things that you can do that are just for your enjoyment?** Discover things that bring you joy and are not about something to do with learning or being productive with your time. Think in the realm of reading a spicy romance novel (or whatever genre you enjoy), blasting your favorite songs and singing at the top of your lungs, or something completely stupid like jumping on the bed.
- **Are there hobbies you would like to try?** A hobby is an activity you do regularly in your leisure time for pleasure. I am going to say that one more time: for pleasure! Not to learn something, not to get in exercise, not to create a side hustle. Do a puzzle, garden, crochet, make jewelry, or bake the recipes you have saved on your phone. You don't have to be good at it, you just need an activity that regularly brings you pleasure. Oh, I would say get your mind out of the gutter but that probably counts as a hobby, too.
- **Who do you enjoy spending time with?** No matter how antisocial you may claim to be, humans are social species by nature. You need time with other adults. Maybe that is

hanging with friends, date night, or time with your mom, sister, cousin, brother. . . .

- **What helps you feel better even if you don't necessarily like doing it?** Yes I am hinting at exercise, sleep, and eating healthier. As much as we may want to deny it, these very basic self-care tasks have a large impact on your overall well-being.
- **In what ways can you be more loving to yourself?** We are our own worst critics, and if you are anything like me, you are probably pretty hard on yourself. Maybe you could use a little more positive self-talk, set boundaries, or say no more often. Being a mom is hard, and we need to find ways to be easier on ourselves.

Again, I am going to remind you that as you go through this process, do not place judgment on anything that you envision for yourself. This is the time to dream, to think out of the box, to challenge yourself in believing what is possible for your life. Write down every little thing that comes to your mind no matter how practical or impractical it may seem to you. If your mind can come up with it, it is something you deserve to make a part of your life.

Once you have completed your lists, take a moment to celebrate that you took the time to think of a long list of things that you want to prioritize for yourself. This is a huge accomplishment, and I hope that you are starting to feel excited about implementing these practices into your life.

SMARTify Your Goals

From the amazing list you envisioned, you are going to start building out SMART self-care practices to incorporate into your life. What the heck does that mean? You are going to make your self-care practices *specific, measurable, attainable, realistic,* and *time bound* based on your individual needs. Why SMART practices? Because these guidelines provide you with the steps it takes to be consistently successful at practicing self-care. They give you the road map by clarifying the what, when, where, why, and how—and the who is obviously you.

Pick five things on your list that you want to focus on. Yes, just five! And choose a couple that are really simple, some in between, and at least one challenging one. I know that seems like a very small amount considering you just listed pages of things you want to do for yourself. But, Momma, remember that we are trying to break the habit of doing all the things. And I know from experience, if you try to pile it all on at once, it will feel more burdensome than helpful, and you will burn out! Don't worry, remember I said that this is a Vegas buffet so you can go back for what you want, whenever you want. You just have to pace yourself and take on a little bit at a time. And if you are having trouble coming up with ideas for practices; remember, there is a list for you at the end of the book.

Let's start with this first round and SMARTify your five self-care practices.

- **Specific**—Is it specifically actionable or did you state a generalized need? Example: getting healthy versus working out three to four days a week at a gym.
- **Measurable**—Does your self-care action have measurable elements: number of days, amount of time, number of times you will perform the action?
- **Achievable**—Is the goal realistic and achievable for you?
- **Relevant**—Is the goal relevant to you, your life, and your self-care practice?

- **Time Bound**—What is a realistic time frame for you to complete or implement the goal?

Specific

One of the biggest mistakes people make when creating goals for themselves is making them vague. There is zero specificity, and people think in terms of big ideas. But big ideas are overwhelming and often lead to psyching yourself out of pursuing your goal. It's like when people look you in your face and tell you, "You need to take better care of yourself." All that does is unleash Pandora's box of all the things you aren't doing right along with all the guilt, anger, and overwhelm. The takeaway: Generalized statements do not help!

If you are starting with a general statement or an idea from your self-care vision like get healthier or rest, or look better in clothes, ask yourself what physical action will I take to accomplish this? Where will I do this? And how do the logistics of getting it done occur when your little crotch goblins monopolize most of your time? For instance, I often hear moms say they want to get healthy. That's a great goal but a very broad idea. There are a ton of different ways to get healthy, so you need to definitively state the physical action you are going to take to make your self-care idea more specific.

Do you want to eat better, work out more, lose weight, or take more vitamins? If it's working out, what kind of workout: weight training, Pilates, walking?

So let's play out the getting healthy example:

What: Get healthier.

How (the action): I am going to weight train.

Where (the tool): At the gym.

Goal: I will get healthier by weight training at the gym.

Or don't be afraid to take your big idea and scale it back.

Goal: I will get healthier by walking outside.

Or, even more scaled back, I have personally found that the smaller I start, the more successful I am.

Goal: I will get healthier by drinking water from my water bottle.

Okay, your turn:

Goal:

Measurable

Now that you have an action you can perform, you are going to quantify it. You have to determine the amount of time you need for the self-care practice you want to incorporate into your life. How often are you going to participate in this self-care practice? How long are you going to do it? Is it something you plan to do daily, weekly, monthly, or annually? And how long will each occurrence take: minutes, hours, days? Or how much do you need: four ounces, eight ounces, five pages, one chapter?

Goal: I will get healthier by weight training at the gym, 6 days a week, for an hour a day.

Or

Goal: I will get healthier by walking outside, 5 days a week, for 45 minutes a day.

Or

Goal: I will get healthier by drinking water, 32 ounces with each meal, totaling 96 ounces.

Okay, your turn:

Goal:

____

____

____

____

____

____

____

Attainable

This is the part where you have to be really honest with yourself. You have to ask yourself, *Do I have the capacity to take this on at this point in my life*? I will say that even your pie-in-the-fucking-sky goals are attainable with time. The key to making your self-care practices attainable is to break them down into smaller steps. And this is where I am going to remind you once again to let go of the all-or-nothing mentality, and I encourage you to start small.

If you don't regularly work out, have a full-time job, a house to run, kids to care for, and more, are you realistically going to be able to suddenly jump from randomly working out one or two times per month to working out at the gym for an hour, six days a week? The answer is probably no. I know this because I can't tell you how many times I have tried to go from zero days a week to a full-week workout schedule only to burn out in about two and a half weeks. So the best thing to do is pare your goals back and set yourself up for success because at the end of the day, a little something is better than a little nothing.

So try this:

Goal: I will get healthier by weight training at the gym, 3 days a week, for 40 minutes a day.

Or

Goal: I will get healthier by walking outside, 3 days a week, 20 minutes a day.

Or

Goal: I will get healthier by drinking water, 8 ounces, four times a day, totaling 32 ounces.

Okay, your turn:

Goal:

Relevant

The question you want to ask yourself is, *Does this work for my life at this time of my life*? Will it serve my needs, align with my priorities, and fit within my current capabilities? That doesn't mean you have to toss a goal out the window. Sometimes you just need an adjustment to make it relevant for you at this time in your life or save it for another time.

You may have added gardening to your vision of self-care practices, but suppose you are the mother of a newborn and currently live in an apartment. Tending to a full-blown garden is probably not something you can take on at this moment, and I am going to guess it won't serve your most immediate needs. That doesn't mean totally give up on the possibility of gardening. You can shelve it for now or maybe start with growing just a couple of herbs on your windowsill.

Maybe you want to get healthier by weight training more, but you can't afford a gym membership, or you are terrified to enter a gym because you know nothing about weight training. You can adjust by starting at home with a set of weights, some free YouTube videos, or a paid app.

If you want to get healthier by walking but it's winter and you live where snow blizzards and negative-degree weather is a common occurrence, start with getting in your steps in your house, at the local mall, or on the stairs at your office.

If you want to get healthier by drinking water but it tastes like the liquid equivalent of air to you, go pick up some water flavor packets or add your favorite fruit to your water so that it has a hint of some flavor.

Making your self-care practice more relevant to your current life situation doesn't make it any less impactful, but it is making it more possible for you to be successful.

So try this:

Goal: I will get healthier by weight training at home with YouTube videos, 3 days a week, for 40 minutes a day.

Or

Goal: I will get healthier by walking the stairs at work, 3 days a week, for 20 minutes a day.

Or

Goal: I will get healthier by drinking water with sliced oranges, 8 ounces, 4 times a day, totaling 32 ounces.

Okay, your turn:

Goal:

____

____

____

____

____

____

____

Time Bound

Time bound means you are going to bind the self-care practice to a particular time. And the more specific you can be, the more likely you will follow through. This is important because it forces you to carve out the time for self-care practices in your extremely demanding schedule, aka making your needs a priority. That's why we are here, right?

It is one of the most necessary steps to help you maintain consistency. You already know that leaving self-care up to the willy-nilly hope that extra time will magically fall in your lap will lead you right back to the hole you are trying to crawl out of.

Try to pick times that already align with your schedule as it exists and are least likely to be affected by change. It can be at a specific time or aligned with a specific activity. You just need to pick predictable times for your self-care practice that you can realistically stick to.

So try this:

Goal: I will get healthier by weight training at home with YouTube videos, Monday, Wednesday, and Friday for 40 minutes after dropping the kids off at school (or 8:30 AM).

Or

Goal: I will get healthier by walking the stairs at work, Monday, Wednesday and Friday, for 20 minutes, after I eat lunch (or at 1:00 PM).

Or

Goal: I will get healthier by drinking water with orange slices, 8 ounces, when I wake up, before I eat breakfast, and with lunch and dinner, totaling 32 ounces.

Okay, your turn:

Goal:

Of course life happens, but carving out the time to implement a self-care practice makes it that much more possible to practice self-care on a regular basis even if it is as small as drinking water throughout the day.

My SMART Self-Care Practices

Take the time to write out your self-care practices using language that is specific, measurable, attainable, relevant, and time bound.

Goal 1

S☐ M☐ A☐ R☐ T☐

Goal 2

S☐ M☐ A☐ R☐ T☐

Goal 3

S☐ M☐ A☐ R☐ T☐

Goal 4

S☐ M☐ A☐ R☐ T☐

Goal 5

S☐ M☐ A☐ R☐ T☐

No matter where you are on the spectrum of a self-care practice, you can walk through SMARTifying any part of your self-care vision, at any time, to help you get really clear about how you can add self-care practices into your life in a viable way. Are you starting to be able to see some form of consistent self-care as a real possibility for yourself? In the next couple of chapters, we are going to expand on ways to create more space in your life for you to prioritize your self-care, but if you can start with the smallest, tiniest thing to begin to implement, you are taking a huge step in the right direction.

CHAPTER 4:

MAKE YOURSELF A PRIORITY:

It's Your Damn Turn

THERE WAS A TIME when I thought that I should be able to do it all. And I ran myself ragged trying to live up to all the standards and expectations I believed existed. And like a lot of moms, I thought self-care was something frivolous and selfish that I didn't have time for. I bought into the idea that motherhood is all about self-sacrifice. I measured my worth in all the things that I did for everyone else and thought that neglecting myself made me more worthy of the "mom" title. How could I possibly make time for myself in between all the things I should be doing for everyone else? Meanwhile, I was burned out, overwhelmed, and I didn't recognize the woman I had become.

It all came to a head one day when I was in a Los Angeles passport office trying to get a passport for my youngest son, who was three months old, so that we could travel to see my husband, who was working in Australia. His mother, who lived in Massachusetts, had passed away; one of my stepdaughters was admitted to a hospital in LA for an autoimmune disease; and I was three months postpartum with my fourth child. In between all of that, I was still momming and managing a house with four kids minus the hands-on, daily support of my husband. Both he and I really needed the support of each other at the time, and I couldn't travel without our infant child.

My husband had to have paperwork signed by some government official in Australia in order to get the passport for our son. The paperwork got lost in the mail for days, and after finally tracking it down to a FedEx office, I managed to get an appointment for the passport the day before I needed to leave. Well, the passport agent took one look at the paperwork and said that the dates didn't match and said he wouldn't be able to give me the passport that day. Not being in my right mind, I didn't realize that the dates written by the Australian official was day/month/year while my husband wrote month/day/year.

Well, as they say, "That was the straw that broke the camel's back." I started sobbing uncontrollably into my son's cloth diaper that I was using as a burp cloth. I had not one single shred of patience, fortitude, or wherewithal left in me. The poor passport agent didn't know what to do. He just stood there profusely apologizing while I loudly sobbed into the burp cloth with my son hovering over the counter in a baby carrier. Eventually, a security guard made his way over to me and escorted me out into the hallway. I was too far gone to even be aware enough to feel any level of embarrassment. In the hallway, I called my husband immediately to explain what happened, but I was a mess and just burst out in some inaudible panic of words that sent my husband into a panic because I almost never cry.

I was a broken, exhausted, overwhelmed mess. I was far beyond my breaking point, and I didn't even have the capacity to see it coming because I was basically a zombie of a person. I had been in an almost six-year cycle of putting everyone else's needs first. I knew I needed more sleep, more downtime, more help, but I kept pushing my feelings to the side and prioritizing everyone else because I thought that's what good mothers do.

It often felt like I was in a perpetual cycle of frantically managing everyone else's needs. There was the regular chaos of everyday life and then there was the constant, unpredictable crap thrown my way all day, every day. . . . One of the kids gets sick, my husband has to unexpectedly go out of town for work, we run out of sandwich meat, somebody left their school project at home, the car breaks down. . . . And the moment I think I can get a moment for myself, life has other ideas, and my needs move to the back burner yet again.

Trying to prioritize my needs seemed to be an impossible task, and I often found myself just giving up. The day-to-day struggle of fitting me into what I needed to get done, what I wanted to get done, and what I actually have the time to get done made me want to throw all of it in the trash, hide under a blanket on the couch, and doom-scroll social media. That inevitably leads to a terrible cycle of stress, mom guilt, a bout of anxiety, and the feeling that I am a complete failure at managing all this crap. Then I punish myself by not doing anything to care for my needs because I don't deserve that time and . . . *Ughhh!!! Why am I like this?*

But here is the inevitable truth: If Mom is not okay, it trickles down into the rest of the family. If I am feeling stressed, anxious, overwhelmed, and on the verge of yelling at everyone for the smallest misstep because my needs haven't been met, I can't be the wife, mom, daughter, friend, and so on, that I want or need to be. And I came to the realization that effectively dealing with all the shit that mom life throws my way has to start with me being mentally, physically, emotionally, socially, and spiritually sound.

Yes, I only said, "sound," aka, in decent condition. Again, you should not be striving for perfection in every area, at all times. That is an impossible standard that will set you up for failure. You already know that there are times when you are killing it at work but failing at momming, times when your kids need your full focus and everything else falls to pieces, and times where it feels like everything in life is pulling you in a hundred different directions. There will always be stress, you will always have feelings like sadness, anger, and anxiety, and it is normal to get tired and overwhelmed. These are facts.

Practicing self-care isn't going to change any of that, because that's just part of life. What self-care does is increase your ability to cope with the crap thrown at you day in and day out while improving your capacity to emotionally regulate through it. It boosts your resilience to help you recover and rebound from stress, overwhelm, and anxiety more quickly. And this calms your nervous system and allows you to spend more time feeling content and calm.

I know that may sound like a tall order right now, like it's a little too far-fetched for your current reality. The benefits of self-care aren't going to happen overnight, just like it takes time to build a new muscle. When strengthening a new muscle, the best thing to do is to slow down and take one small step at a time, one small victory at a time. You are shooting for long-term success with self-care and not the quick fix of doing it all right now. You can't run at full speed, nonstop all the time. Keep it slow and steady.

You don't have to be a superhero or self-sacrificing martyr to be a good mom. In fact, I would argue the exact opposite. You can't be the best version of yourself if your needs are constantly neglected. Yes, most of us manage most of the time, but eventually the stress bubbles over, and it's only a matter of time before you crash and burn. Mommy brain kicks into full drive, and the next thing you know your cell phone ends up in your dresser drawer, your keys are in the refrigerator, and you are crying on the living room floor because you are now late, you yelled at your kid, and you can't find anything because you have hit your limit.

I realized that I wasn't going to be able to manage being a mother of four kids, a stepmom, a wife, a daughter, an employee, a sister—all the roles I had—if I didn't start prioritizing my needs and taking better care of myself. But how the hell was I going to find the time for me? How was I going to fit something else into my already overfilled, chaotic days when I was struggling with managing things as they were?

Start Small

By the time I had given into the fact that I needed more self-care in my life, I had no idea where to begin. I was overwhelmed, and it had been so long since I had considered my own needs that I was at a loss. I am not a meditating type of girl, and the idea of doing yoga on the floor while my kids climbed all over me just made me feel overstimulated. I wasn't in the headspace to journal, and taking walks meant I would also have to walk with a stroller, an infant, a toddler, and a dog. *No, thanks!* I just wanted to find something small that required little of me but that I could enjoy for myself.

I used to be such an avid reader, and I really missed getting lost in a good book. So trying my hand at reading seemed like a small, simple step in the right direction. I figured I get in bed every single night and scroll social media on my phone anyway, so I decided I was going to read in bed instead before I went to sleep. I bought a book and put it on my bedside table. Most nights I only read about five to ten minutes, and I was lucky to read more than a few pages before the book fell from my hands and smacked me in the face. My husband thought it was hilarious and was usually the one who would turn off my lamp, take the book off my face, and place it back on the bedside table.

Some books I loved, and some I absolutely hated, but I eventually found a few genres that I kept returning to. I didn't give a shit about reading goals, I wasn't trying to learn something from any self-help gurus, and I definitely didn't want to read any books that required anything of me beyond basic reading skills. I am going to keep it real and let you know that the majority of the books I read are complete smut. And you can judge me if you want to, but I found immense joy in my new hobby. And you know what? I started to notice some changes: My brain tended to turn off when I was reading, I got to sleep much faster, my quality of sleep was better, and best of all, those smutty books helped me get my libido back. Now you will almost always find me with some form of a book in hand. I have over forty books in my bedroom, I always carry my Kindle with me when I am out and about, and I listen to an audiobook while I walk, clean, cook, or drive.

It's probably been a long time since you have made an effort to practice self-care. I am going to guess it feels like you are going against everything you have been taught about being a mother, whether consciously or subconsciously. Or maybe it feels like you are so overwhelmed by motherhood you can't see past just surviving the day. If the idea of starting even the smallest, simplest act of self-care feels overwhelming to you, I want you to know that I get it! But I want to encourage you to give it a try and start with something small.

What's something simple you used to do that you miss? Let's start with the lowest-hanging fruit. Take a look at your amazing list of SMARTified self-care practices and pick a really easy one to implement that you think you can actually enjoy. Maybe it's reading, doing a puzzle, being outside, baking? Is there an easy way to incorporate a simple self-care practice into your existing routine? Can you crochet while watching TV? Listen to an audiobook while cleaning or driving? Take a walk outside after lunch? Maybe you have an area where you can keep a puzzle out and do it for ten minutes while you drink your morning coffee or after the witching hour to help calm your mind.

I want you to try to keep this as enjoyable and simple as possible. If your list isn't working for you, refer to the self-care ideas listed at the end of the book. And if even that feels like too much, try starting with the simple act of brain dumping. Get a notebook and, when your brain goes into overdrive, write down all the to-dos and worries that come up for you. The key is to try out some place to start. And remember if it doesn't work for you, you can pick something else and try again. You can try three, ten, or thirty practices until you find the simple thing that clicks for you.

Some of you may be reading this thinking that reading for fun or taking a ten-minute walk is not going to do a damn thing to combat the stress you feel. I hear you! But this is about building a foundation for basic self-care, and you have to start with simple tasks you can slowly implement into your routine so as not to overwhelm yourself. If you try to do it all at once, you will burn out. And frankly, a collection of small actions can have a much larger impact than you think.

It's okay if you are looking at the self-care practices you listed in Chapter 3 and you realize you need to rethink and simplify even more. Maybe you need to make it as simple as a hot shower, a short nap, or sitting down to eat at least one meal a day. I know people say that things like showering or having a meal is not self-care. But don't listen, because these things are the very foundation of self-care.

If you are a new mom who is constantly covered in spit-up or some other bodily fluid, a daily shower can feel like the most luxurious level of self-care that exists. If you are dealing with depression or crippling anxiety, taking a nap may be the break your brain needs during tough days. If you find yourself surviving off peanut butter and jelly crust, stolen chicken nuggets, and random fruit your kid suddenly despises, eating a meal with "adult" food might become the highlight of your day.

Make Habits Stackable

The second thing I want you to do is find a regular part of your daily routine where you can attach that new self-care practice. This is what is called "habit stacking," and it has become one of the most surefire techniques that I use to successfully add self-care practices to my crazy days. I didn't invent this term; I'm pretty sure I heard it on a podcast or some book I read along the way, but I do remember my scattered brain having a lightbulb moment when I was introduced to the technique of habit stacking.

Let's walk through this together. Pick one or two simple self-care practices that you SMARTified in Chapter 3. The goal is to keep it simple and start where you are.

Once you have chosen a simple, potentially enjoyable self-care practice, you are going to "stack" or group it with a regular part of your daily routine. Here is the good news. For the most part, you already have a basic routine to your day, a rhythm by which you function—and if you didn't already know this, I hope it became obvious to you when you tracked all that you do in Chapter 2. I want you to take a moment to look over that schedule or routine of yours and make note of the things you consistently do.

What time are you getting up? Do you have coffee every morning? Do you eat breakfast? Drink tea? Do you take your kids to school or daycare? What's your work schedule like? What's your midday routine? If you pick up your kids, what time do you typically do that? How often are you in the car? What is the after-school schedule? Homework? Dinnertime? Bedtime? You get the drift. You are looking for patterns and consistency because that is the groundwork for stacking new habits. If you did a good job of SMARTifying your task in Chapter 3, this work may already be done. But if you need to, it's no big deal to make adjustments.

Like I mentioned, I stacked reading with my sleep routine. As soon as my head hits the pillow, I pick up a book and begin reading, which quiets my chaotic mind (that never seems to shut the fuck up), and about fifteen to thirty minutes later I drift off into a sound sleep. For you this could be going on a walk right after lunch, crocheting while you watch TV, or napping in your car while your kids are at their activities. The goal is to create cues for self-care throughout the day by stacking simple practices with your regular routine.

The last step to making this successful is doing a little preplanning. I keep an array of fun, spicy romance novels in a few different subgenres on my nightstand. Keeping those books immediately accessible even if I am laying down all but guarantees I will follow through with this form of self-care. If you want to nap in your car, toss a neck pillow and travel blanket in your trunk. If you want to crochet while watching TV, keep a basket of your supplies next to where you watch TV.

Warning. Warning. It may take a while for you to figure out the best way to stack a particular practice with your daily routine. Your first attempt may look great on paper but fails miserably in action. That's not a sign that you failed. It just means you need to make some adjustments and give it another try.

For instance, your SMART practice may have been something along the lines of "Take my vitamins daily in the morning and at night." And I can tell you this is something I struggled with a lot, because I regularly forgot, and then I would fall off taking them for months at a time. But being a forty-plus woman in perimenopause, vitamins have become a necessity, so I had to figure out a way to trigger my brain to remember to take my vitamins. I started with putting them in a cabinet in the kitchen and thought I would take them with breakfast, but that didn't work. I put them on the bathroom counter so I could see them and take them at nighttime, and that didn't work.

I realized, for my scattered mind, I needed to get much more specific around the habit of taking my vitamins as part of stacking. One thing I never forget to do in the morning is drink coffee. So now my vitamins are on the kitchen counter right in my eyeline next to my Nespresso machine. And as my coffee brews, I put all my morning vitamins in a small bowl and then bring my coffee, breakfast, and vitamins to the table. That consistently works for me.

At night, I fill my water bottle before I go upstairs. When I open the fridge for ice, that is the trigger to take my liquid vitamins like omegas and vitamin D that I store in the fridge. And finally (yes, I have to take a lot of damn vitamins) when I get in bed, I keep any nighttime pills like magnesium on my bedside table (next to the spicy books), so even if I am cozy in the bed, they are right at my fingertips along with water to take them.

I still forget from time to time and probably will never be perfect at taking my vitamins. However, I am not striving for perfection because I have come to terms with the fact that it will never happen. And I strongly feel that constantly striving for perfection is the biggest obstacle to overcome. That all-or-nothing mentality is what made me give up on even trying. Consistency over perfection is the key to success.

As you can see, it was a multistep process to play around with what worked and figure out the best tasks or practices to stack my vitamins onto to make me successful at adding that care practice to my life. I finally found what works, and I have been able to consistently maintain taking my vitamins. I now take my vitamins about 85 percent of the time. I feel better, I have more energy, and I am mentally, physically, and emotionally a little healthier from one self-care practice.

As you step up your game and become more comfortable with prioritizing yourself, challenge yourself to habit stack more difficult self-care practices that fit your needs. Think about daily, weekly, monthly, and even annual practices you can slowly add. Try implementing stretching for ten minutes before you go to bed at night and give yourself a couple of weeks to figure out a stretch routine that works for you. If you want to add meal planning and prep to your weekends to follow through on eating healthier meals during the week, give yourself about a month to work through the logistics. Make your birthday the day you call to make all your annual doctors' appointment for things like your gynecological exam, mammogram, eye checkup, and dental cleaning. I know it's an annoying task, but perceive it as giving yourself the gift of health every year. Keep going until you reach a point where you feel that the majority of your needs are being met, on a regular basis, without feeling overwhelmed.

Practice Patience

As you move through this process, I want you to be patient and focus on consistency over perfection. That means you have to come to terms with the fact that you will never be perfect at your self-care practice. You will forget, things will come up, and life will happen. None of that means you are a failure; it just means you are human. So, when you inevitably forget, miss a few times, or check out for the week because you are exhausted, none of that undoes the work you have already done. Just start again and shoot for consistency.

When you mess up, feelings like anger, frustration, and maybe even defeat are going to come up for you. The goal is to be able to acknowledge the feeling without following through with punishing yourself for the perceived failure. If you find you are chastising yourself with negative self-talk, follow up with more compassionate self-talk. If you realize you are punishing yourself by deserting your practices, avoiding downtime, or canceling things because you feel like you don't deserve self-care, double down on the acts of self-care you find yourself avoiding.

For instance, when you hear that negative voice in your head going on about how awful you are for giving in to your craving for cake and you should just binge out for the rest of the week because you ruined everything, reframe the negative talk and remind yourself that one slice of cake will *never* undo a week of healthy eating. Then get right back to making healthier choices. Or if you find yourself canceling a night out with your girlfriends because you didn't finish the household chores or feel like you didn't spend enough time with your kids or spouse or whoever, add an extra hour to your hangout time because you most likely need it even more if you are in the mode of punishing yourself. These kinds of corrections help you relearn how to respond to yourself with patience rather than punishment.

This process may take you a few months to fully implement, or it could take a couple of years. Yes, I said *years*. This is just the beginning of a learning process. You are learning about yourself and how to better serve your needs, and you are unlearning practices and beliefs that have been harmful to your well-being. All this takes time and patience. The goal is to trust the process, trust yourself, and keep taking small steps to build a sustainable self-care practice that works for you. Like they say, "Rome wasn't built in a day," and you for damn sure won't change your self-care practice overnight.

CHAPTER 5:

STOP DOING IT ALL:
Tell Super Mom Syndrome to Go to Hell

WE LIVE IN A WORLD where moms are bombarded with a "perfect version" of motherhood day after day through filtered squares on social media. We see an endless stream of immaculately organized houses, color-coordinated playrooms, the cutest lunches with perfectly balanced nutrition, over-the-top birthday parties, and impeccable mom style that can all be pulled off in "just a few simple steps." We are all pinning, tweeting, Facebooking, Instagramming, and TikToking to the point that we have become driven by the delusional belief that mothers are somehow capable of doing all the things for all the people in their life, at all times, while perfectly managing their own needs. And this, my friend, is called Super Mom Syndrome.

So what are the signs that you may be suffering from Super Mom Syndrome? One is that you are a mom. Hahaha, just kidding—not really. But on a serious note: Do the littlest things irritate the shit out of you? Are you constantly forgetting things for you? Do you feel like you are in a constant state of fog? Do you have unexplainable mood swings? Do you avoid interactions like hanging out or simply returning a text or e-mail? Does making yet another decision overwhelm you? Is your anxiety easily triggered? Do you feel resentment toward others? Are your back and neck muscles in knots? Do you regularly get headaches? Do you feel like you have no time for yourself and when you do finally get time you are too overwhelmed to do anything for yourself? When things don't go as planned, are you quick to punish and berate yourself for not upholding these fantastical standards?

And one of the biggest signs you are suffering from Super Mom Syndrome is mom guilt! You find yourself in a constant cycle of trying to do it all, then overcompensating for all the things you perceive you didn't do enough of, followed by beating yourself up for not getting it right the first time, and then giving yourself zero credit for the things you did get right. It's a vicious cycle moms fall into based on a harmful, bullshit belief of what motherhood should look like. And it results in the terrible symptoms of negative self-talk and neglectful practices that keep us in the chronic Super Mom Syndrome cycle.

You might be wondering where all this comes from. Society has bamboozled you into believing that you by yourself should be able to raise children like a stay-at-home mom yet work full-time, plan and manage every minute of your kids' lives while maintaining a social life of your own, work out daily and have a side hustle, eat a diet filled with organic and homemade meals, keep up with friendships, be a sex kitten in the bedroom, drink water, get outside, journal regularly, read in your spare time, and pick up a hobby like knitting or gardening—all with a grateful smile on your face (insert emoji of strained smile). And whatever a partner can contribute is just icing on the cake.

You try your best to parent through roller-coaster days of constantly being on the offensive to deal with any stressors, issues, or conflicts. You referee ridiculous fights, negotiate tantrums, regulate emotions, and redirect behavior, all while managing the basic standards of clothing, feeding, bathing, and getting the kiddos where they have to go—not to mention keeping your home running, self-regulating so you can be a present and effective parent, and bearing the weight of the invisible motherload. And don't forget to keep up with how to gently and holistically parent your securely attached child as consciously as possible while still allowing them autonomy. Oh, and you are still expected to have the qualities of a momma bear, tiger mom, and lawn-mower parent (wait, I think that's the bad one).

Then there are the "extra" things that get piled on top of all the to-dos already on our list: Saying yes to something you know you really don't have the time for or don't even want to do in the first place, like joining the PTA or volunteering to make hats for the school play. Or planning an over-the-top themed birthday party for your toddler that takes over your life for three months simply because you feel obligated. And don't forget to take those three bags in your trunk to Goodwill, buy a birthday present for the thirty-seventh birthday party your kid was invited to this month, pick up a tie-dye shirt for spirit week, and buy individually wrapped snacks for the soccer team that are sugar-free, nut-free, and gluten-free.

Holy freakin' crap! I don't know about you, but even after just reading that, my shoulders are tensed up to my ears, and I can feel myself grinding my teeth. And if you are anything like me, in your real, everyday life, laundry and dishes pile up, homework is forgotten, to-do lists go unchecked, e-mails go unanswered, and it feels like you are falling apart at the seams. You hide your imperfections and struggles like they are some terrible secret affliction you need to exorcise and suffer in silence because you are convinced you are the only mom out there struggling to keep it all together.

You are not alone! Every time someone tells me I am a super mom, I just want to scream, "THAT'S NOT A COMPLIMENT!" I am not a super mom, and that statement not only dismisses how hard being a mom really is, but it also makes it seem as if women have access to some magical power that makes it possible when really we are all stressing ourselves out trying to live up to impossible standards. I mean, I do think I have a superpower or two, like super hearing, but for the most part I am just a human being doing everything in my power to get through the day-to-day challenges of parenting my little crotch goblins.

I have always been the type of person who does too much. And after my passport office meltdown, you would have thought I learned my lesson. But nooooo . . . I thought I could still manage all the things and as long as I just sprinkled my day with some self-care practices, I would be good. I could wake up an hour early for me time, meditate, work out six days a week, prioritize productivity throughout my day, add another side hustle, get the to-do list done, drink water, eat right, cart the kids here and there, and so on and so forth. But I couldn't shake the constant feelings of stress, overwhelm, and exhaustion, and all I could think was, *What is wrong with me that I can't manage being productive at work, a present and proactive mom with my kids, and easily manage the ins and outs of daily life?*

I kept pushing and pushing to get it right. It finally felt like I hit my stride when the pandemic came along. The extracurricular activities were down to a bare minimum, my kids were home most of the time, and the school day was contained within my home. It was a miracle because it felt like I had more control of my time, and the dream of balancing my life seemed just within reach. I started getting up before the kids to meditate and work out, I landed my dream job as a staff writer for one of my fav websites, and I was finally hitting my income goals in my business. I was managing "virtual" school for four kids, all of whom had additional educational support services included in their IEPs or 504s, making home-cooked meals, and painting with Bob Ross videos on PBS at the end of the day to relax.

I was doing it. I had finally figured it all out and was managing the ideal life "balance" [insert maniacal laugh]. Then the next school year came along, and I found out my kids would still be doing some cross scheduling between in-person and virtual schooling for an unknown amount of time and the schedules were an awful, chaotic mess. I was lacking sleep because I was staying up until 2:00 AM to meet the unbelievable amount of deadlines I had. I could feel the panic of managing it all start to rise.

The next thing I knew, I was spending afternoons rocking on the floor in my closet while stuffing my face with whatever snack I could get my hands on, trying my damnedest to regulate very chaotic emotions that I couldn't seem to get under control. To this day I can feel the remnants of the burning sensation of cortisol coursing through my veins and the agitated, unwelcomed high I got from it. My sanity was imploding a little bit every day, and I denied it until it couldn't be ignored. I was in the throes of Super Mom Syndrome, and it went on for almost two years.

In December 2022, my husband had to go on a work trip, and I threatened his life to make him bring me with him (just kidding/not really). By that point, I was numb, exhausted, and practically in a zombie state, but life was moving too fast for me to recognize what was happening. I spent that trip sleeping, eating, and roaming the streets of a foreign town in a daze. I finally had a moment to take stock of the state I was in, and it wasn't good.

I figured I just needed some downtime to rest and then I could get back on my "mom boss" schedule after the holidays. Well, the holidays came and went, and I could not summon one ounce of energy or a single fuck to care about anything. I had no energy, no focus, no motivation, no libido, nothing. I was doing the bare minimum to get by and keep my family and home running. I kept thinking I just needed a little push to get going, but my mind and body were telling me I needed to stop doing all the damn things, and I just wouldn't listen. Then my dog passed away, I twisted my ankle and ended up in a boot for six weeks, and we had to temporarily move into a much smaller rental home with all four kids in one bedroom. Now the universe was forcing me to go sit my behind down somewhere and I had no choice but to do it.

I finally acquiesced to it all and reached out to a therapist. I told her all the reasons my body had shut down, and why I probably needed to be diagnosed with ADHD, and how I just needed her to give some type of regime or medication so I could get it together. She patiently listened to me go on and on about all the things I was failing at managing and how I needed to get better at scheduling and organizing my life. After I rambled on for a few sessions, she stopped me and told me she was pretty sure this wasn't caused by ADHD. Based on what I was telling her, she was officially diagnosing me with "clinical burnout."

I went into immediate denial. *Clinical burnout! I can't be burned out because I was doing all the self-care things. I'd already been through this, and I know better, so there is no way this is happening again! I know better!* My therapist told me to "breathe." She gave me a homework assignment to think about who or what was requiring me to do all the things that I had listed out to her? Who or what was holding me accountable to all these expectations?

Shit! I had become the poster child for Super Mom Syndrome. I had become the person who set myself up with unrealistic expectations that no one else was holding me to. I had experienced mom burnout multiple times, and during those times I was constantly on the edge of being angry. Anything could set me off, and when my anger exploded it would hit anyone within striking distance even if they weren't at fault: my kids, husband, family members, the person who failed to put on their turn signal (yes, I have road-rage issues). And then the inevitable mom guilt would come along, and I would punish myself by withholding care practices for myself. I didn't know how to get out of this cycle.

Have you ever stopped to explore the expectations you feel are being placed on you? Whose standards are you living your life by? Are you really not good enough, or has society made it so that you will never think you are good enough? I would argue that at least 95 percent of what you are feeling is completely unjustified because you are comparing yourself to a fictional version of a mother who doesn't exist. Unfortunately, it is once again up to moms to change the narrative, which starts with putting your cape down and dropping the illusion that you are some kind of superhero.

How? Here is where you pause and reevaluate the expectations you hold for yourself and how you deal with them. This is where you start the practice of letting go of outside expectations and redefining what you want your motherhood journey to look like for yourself. How do you do that? Identify your priorities, define enforceable boundaries, say no and mean it, and ask for help and learn to accept it.

Breaking out of Super Mom Syndrome is simple, but I won't pretend that it is easy. It is sometimes easier to fall into the trap of doing everything yourself because no one else does it right. But who is that serving? No one. It alienates your parenting partner, perpetuates that illusion that you are fine handling it all, keeps you from asking for help that you so desperately need, and breeds anger and resentment. That cycle stops right now—starting today.

Identify Priorities

You already did the work to name everything that you manage, think about, and do in all the roles you play. The next step is to identify what is actually important to you in your life. I am talking about getting clear on the big-picture priorities for the life you want for yourself and your family. Identifying priorities will give you the framework you need to guide your daily decisions of the what, when, where, and how you will spend your time, energy, and mental capacity.

Your time and well-being are your most precious commodities. As hard as you may try, you already know you can't create more time in the day. And although you may like to believe otherwise, your emotional, mental, physical, spiritual, and social capacities are not infinite. You have limits. (Everyone else does too, no matter how it seems.) It is up to you to guard your capacity so that it can be used in the most beneficial way for you and your family. You can't keep giving the best of you away to everybody and everything else and not saving any for yourself or the things that are important to you.

Look, life happens. That's it. Nothing you do will stop the chaos train from running. Something always has to be sacrificed, but that something doesn't always have to be you. Setting priorities provides you with a framework to make better choices when it comes to how you function within the chaos of motherhood. Without clear priorities, you aimlessly make harried decisions that waste your time and energy on things that are not important to you and only compound your stress, worry, and overwhelm.

Ask yourself: What do happiness and success look like for you at this point in your life? What are the goals, values, and activities *you* deem most important? Not what should be important to you. Not what your parents or in-laws think should matter to you. Not what society says you should prioritize. What is important to you?

Maybe you are a new mom and need to focus on building the bond between you and your baby and rediscovering this new person you are becoming. Maybe you have found your stride as a mom and need to focus more on your self-care practices, mental health, and finding something fun for yourself. Or you could be in a phase of life where you want to focus on strengthening your marriage and building friendships outside of motherhood. Your priorities should be unique to you and based on not only what you want and need but also your current season of life .

Pick up to six priorities to focus on. That doesn't mean you aren't going to ever address things outside of these priorities. It just means that this is where you are focusing your time and energy at this point in your life. These priorities will act as a guide for defining boundaries such as knowing when to say no and determining what kind of help to ask for. If you don't know where to start, here's a list of potential priorities for you to consider. What resonates with you?

Family	Travel
Work	Personal Development/Learning
Exercise	Career
Friends	Hobbies
Education	Parenting
Religious/Spiritual Practice	Relationship
Marriage	Fun
Health	Rest
Finances	Transitioning
Self-Care	
Mental Health	

Once you have chosen your priorities, you are going to rank them in order of importance.

1. ________________________
2. ________________________
3. ________________________
4. ________________________
5. ________________________
6. ________________________

Assigning a hierarchy to your priorities provides you with the framework to make decisions moving forward to manage your time and energy. In other words, you don't need to do every damn thing for every-damn-body. You are not capable of getting everything done all the time, but you are definitely capable of getting the important things done on time. It just takes figuring out what is important to you.

Placing equal importance on everything keeps you in a reactive state of overwhelm. You are just running around in fight-or-flight mode with cortisol pulsing through your veins trying to address anything and everything hurled your way. But the goal is to become proactive rather than reactive and save you from all the stress and anxiety that comes with spreading yourself way too thin.

It's okay if you don't have the answers right away. This may take a little time and self-reflection to figure out. But I want you to think of this as a learning process where nothing is fixed. Your priorities can and will shift based on your changing needs and your season of life.

Define Boundaries

Feelings of overwhelm, resentment, and burnout all come from being mentally, emotionally, and physically exhausted from always playing the super mom role. The only way you can stop that train from running you over is to put blockades in the way—and that, my friend, is what boundaries are for. The very foundation of self-care is setting boundaries because they give you and others the parameters needed to protect your well-being.

Once you have done the work of identifying your priorities, defining boundaries becomes that much easier because now you know what is important to you. Therefore, you can easily identify what you have to do, what you want to do, and most importantly, what you won't do. And you can set the boundaries you need to protect your time, energy, and mental capacity.

I know it is hard to create boundaries and even harder to hold those boundaries with loved ones like your spouse, kids, friends, family members, and even yourself. And admitting you have physical, mental, or emotional boundaries that prevent you from doing it all can feel like an admission of failure. But the truth is the only thing you are failing is yourself when you refuse to take the steps to protect your well-being.

Setting boundaries isn't selfish. Setting boundaries helps you show up at your best when and where you want or need to show up. Simply put, boundaries are routines, habits, and limits that provide safeguards that empower you to maintain your mental, physical, emotional, and spiritual well-being. Seems easy, but how can you set boundaries when you don't know where to start? You actually already did the work, and whether you know it or not, your boundaries already exist.

Guided by your stated priorities, I am going to ask you to refer back to your very long to-do lists and categorize them into four categories: Must Do, Delegate/Transfer, Outsource, Drop. This list will help determine the to-dos in your life that need to be your priority, what you can pass on to someone else, things that can be outsourced, and what can be dropped from the list. And this will begin the journey of dropping that bitch of Super Mom Syndrome from your life.

Must-Dos

Must-dos are the to-dos that only you can do or that you truly want to do. If you are breastfeeding an infant, clearly that needs to be on your must-do list. If you find immense joy in cooking a big Sunday dinner for your family, add it to the list. Showing up for work is something only you can do. Reading bedtime stories to your kids might also be a nonnegotiable for you. Your self-care routines: always on the must-do list.

Yes, I am telling you to make not only your have-to-dos but also your want-to-dos a part of your must-do list. Why want to-dos? Because all too often, moms take off our lists the things that bring us happiness and joy. Then we complain that we never get to do anything for ourselves. So I am telling you now: The things you want to do need to be a nonnegotiable priority because your needs and happiness are just as important as everyone else's!

The must-do list can get very long very quickly. However, the most important part of the must-do list is simplifying it as much as possible. In other words, maybe the question should be, *What can I cut from my must-do list*?—because I guarantee that you are hanging on for dear life to tasks that you can release. If you don't absolutely have to do it yourself or don't absolutely want to do it, it is *not* a must-do.

Transfer or Delegate

These are the to-dos that you hand over to someone or something else. Remember the difference between transferring and delegating. Delegating is when you pass off a task to someone else in your family or household, but you are still the primary manager of said task. Think of chores that the kids need to complete, or you may put older kids in charge of informing you of their schedules for sports or school.

Transferring means you hand the entire task over to another person: the full responsibility of planning, doing, and following up to make sure the task is completed correctly. This may be handing over meal preparation (including grocery shopping), overseeing school communication (e.g., the twenty-five e-mails, four apps, and three daily school calls), or chores such as laundry or dishes. In my home, anyone over age ten is responsible for their own laundry. I hate laundry, and there is no reason I should be the only person in my household spending hours a day to make sure everyone else has clean clothes.

This is something you need to do in partnership with those you are sharing the load with, whether it's a quick discussion or a family meeting. Fair warning: Not everyone is going to be gung-ho about the changes, and that's fine. But the trick is that you have to learn to let go and let whoever you assigned the task to do it the way they choose to do it. Yes, you will need to teach your kids how to do certain things—and God forbid, you may even have to instruct your spouse or partner. However, you can't assign the task and then micromanage how it gets done. I know that can be hard, but you have to hand it over totally so that it no longer takes up space on your already overly full plate.

Outsource

Outsourcing is when you can pay or barter with someone or something else to do a task. These are the to-dos that need to get done, but the cost benefit of someone else doing it far outweighs the use of your time to do it. It may be budgeting to send your laundry out weekly or to hire a housekeeper once a month for deep cleaning. And don't just think of people to outsource to. Also consider grocery shopping with Instacart or using Subscribe & Save on Amazon to auto-order the essentials for your household without having to think about it. It could even be as simple as purchasing a robot vacuum to clean the floors while you do something else.

Yes, finances play a role in your ability to outsource, but some ways to outsource won't break the bank and may even relieve your budget. Try carpooling with another family that goes to the same school or after-school activities as your kids. That means less driving and less gas for you. Or sign your kid up for the free after-school program at school. There is less pressure for you to pick them up by a certain time, and your kid gets activities and homework help at no cost to you. It just takes a little thought and planning to come up with ways you can best outsource to-dos to free up your time and energy.

Drop

These to-dos don't need to be done—by you, or anyone, at any time. They are the things that you feel like you should do but carry no importance or value to you in your life. Or maybe someone has told you it's important, but really it's just a time suck that serves no purpose. And sometimes the level of stress that it causes is just not worth your effort.

It could be matching socks, signing your kids up for *all* the after-school sports activities, or hanging out with certain "friends." For me, it's the PTA. It's a time suck that I absolutely despise. I don't care who judges me, but I will never sign up for it again in my mothering life.

Consider this your call to drop the things that have no significance in your life. I am giving you full permission to drop-kick right out the door all the things you don't give a shit about or that annoy the shit out of you (as long as that kick doesn't negatively affect you). And guess what. I want you to do it with zero guilt. I want you to be so appalled that you allowed those things to take up space in your life that you never allow yourself to add them to your load ever again!

Essentially, the key to breaking your to-do list into these categories is figuring out what you can let go of. What are you going to unload from your plate and maintain the boundary so that it doesn't end up back on there?

Enforcing Boundaries

Figuring out your boundaries is a pretty easy process, but enforcing those boundaries is not. People are going to test your boundaries—your kids, your partner, your parents, your in-laws, friends, and even you. Yes, you will test your own boundaries. You may have to step out of your comfort zone to act on enforcing your boundaries, especially if you are used to constantly accommodating other people's needs over yours. And it can be scary for you not only to communicate your boundary but also to act on it and reinforce it when necessary. This is going to take a little practice and a touch of mental fortitude that may be out of your norm.

First, communicate your new expectations to anyone you are sharing the load with. Once you have made an expectation clear, it is up to each person when, where, and how they meet it. Meanwhile, your job is to set the boundary for what you will and won't accept. Expectations are external, and you have little to no control over how someone will react to your expectation, whereas boundaries are an internal limit that you can choose. You can't control how people respond to your expectations, but you can control when, where, and how you enforce your boundaries.

How do you even start enforcing boundaries when you are so used to just doing things for yourself? Two words: "no" and "help." That's all. Asking for help and saying no are the tools you need to start confidently reinforcing your boundaries so that you can focus on your priorities. Yes, this is a very simplistic approach that doesn't nearly cover all the ways you may need to enforce your boundaries. But it is a straightforward and concrete way to start.

Say No

Moms are socialized to be the know-all, do-all, be-all: super moms. It just takes one scroll of social media to see why moms are so often guilted into feeling like our job is to make sure everyone in our life feels happy and cared for regardless of how we may be struggling. Saying no can be scary, especially if you are used to being the person who everyone turns to for help, the one who picks up everyone's slack at home, the one who is always guilted into saying yes.

When should you say no? When it is not a priority on your list. No matter how much you feel you "should" do something, you need to say no. No, I can't join the PTA. . . . No, I can't join the church planning committee. . . . No, I won't be able to attend the work happy hour after my work hours. . . . No, I can't sign up for another after-school activity.

If a yes will cost you your well-being, then your answer should be an immediate no. And if you feel the stress and resentment start to build up after you gave a yes, you are allowed to retract it. One time I volunteered to host my daughter's soccer team's end-of-the-year party. I don't know why I opened my mouth, but as soon as I did, I immediately started to regret it because I had put too much on my plate. I felt awful, but I had to renege my yes. And guess what. It was no problem. The coach understood and had no problem and was able to find a new location.

What are three things you can say no to right now? Can you back out of PTA or other volunteer commitments? Is there a household chore you can completely transfer to another household member? Is there an extracurricular activity you can quit?

1. ______________________________

____

2. ______________________________

____

3. ______________________________

____

You have to say no and stick to it. It will be difficult in the beginning, and you may feel guilty for exercising your ability to say no. But follow through, and I promise it will get easier with each "no" you say.

Ask for Help

First and foremost, know that asking for help is neither a sign of weakness nor a reason to torture yourself with mom guilt. And maybe you have some control issues that you need to put in check (giving myself side eye on this one). You don't have to be able to do it all to be a good mother. It may be hard to let things go and allow people to step up to help where they are needed. This can be true in your home, at work, in your church community or school setting, and throughout your daily life. As a mom, it is so often easier just to do it yourself, so that it's done the "right" way. In the short term, that may be true, but that is a surefire way to breed overwhelm, resentment, and anger.

Take a moment to think about if your kiddo is trying to do something that makes them feel overwhelmed or stressed, that they feel they can't handle on their own. Would you berate them for not being able to do it? Would you see them as a bad kid or failure because they didn't accomplish said task? Would you punish them by taking away an after-school activity or time with their friends because they needed help? *No!* You would encourage them to ask for help. You would let them know that nobody can do everything on their own. You would do everything in your power to help them. And you would most likely praise them for asking for help. So why not give yourself the same grace? As a fellow mom who still suffers from bouts of Super Mom Syndrome, I know what it's like to struggle with asking for help. It's not something you will master overnight, and you may need a map to guide you down this less traveled path. Here are a few tips to guide you in your quest for help:

- **Identify where you need the help.** And this is the easy part because you have already done the work of figuring out where you need someone else's assistance. But you may also have times where you struggle with your own must-do list, and I encourage you to ask for help then too.
- **Start with a low-risk request.** You can start with something as simple as asking for assistance with loading your groceries in the car when you have kids with you. Or maybe you ask everyone in the house to spend ten minutes a night picking up before bedtime so it's not all on you.
- **Have a specific ask.** People don't do well with general asks and will avoid doing a task because they aren't clear about what you want. Instead of giving instructions such as "You kids need to help clean up around here," try a more specific request like "I need you to be in charge of taking out the trash every day." Or ask a friend or relative to watch your kids for you one time a month so that you and your significant other can have a date night.

- **Accept the help.** Sometimes help is staring you right in the face and you ignore the opportunity because you don't want people to judge you. *Girl! Take the damn help!* If someone is offering, say yes.
- **Show appreciation.** A little thanks can go a long way. When people feel valued or recognized, they will be much more inclined to help the next time you ask, or God forbid, they may take on that task without you even asking.

I am going to force your hand a little bit here because asking for help tends to be really difficult for a lot of moms. So I want you to list three things where you are going to ask for help. Can you ask another mom to carpool so that you don't have to drive all over every day picking up and dropping off kids? Is it possible for a relative or friend to trade off watching kids on a Saturday night so you both can get a date night or some time to yourselves?

1. ______________________________

   ____

2. ______________________________

   ____

3. ______________________________

   ____

Will you struggle with asking for help? For sure, especially when it's not your habit. Will you have to follow up on your request for help? Sometimes, especially when people aren't used to you asking something of them. Will some people disappoint you? Absolutely, but that doesn't mean everyone will, so keep asking. Will there be a day when you can stop asking for help? *No*!

Now I am going to say the thing that a lot of people don't say when addressing moms asking for help: Sometimes you shouldn't have to ask for help! Your spouse, partner, or coparent should share in the responsibilities of raising your child(ren) together and carry part of the mental load. For those of you who don't have a parenting partner to share the load of parenting, I want to acknowledge how deeply unfair it is that you have been put in a situation where you are doing this alone or the majority of heavy lifting is being imposed on you.

I won't lie to you. No matter your situation, asking for help is going to be as uncomfortable as hell when you start. But the more you practice it, the easier it gets. And if you keep avoiding it like I did, life will eventually put you in a position to force your hand. Enforcing boundaries will be an ongoing, daily practice that will change and evolve as life changes. But the more you do it, the more self-aware you will become, and then saying no and passing things off to other people will become second nature, and you will end up feeling more super by the day.

CHAPTER 6:

BUILD SUPPORT: Create Your Own Damn Village

FAIR WARNING: This is the longest chapter in the book because I truly believe building a village to support you is one of the most important things you can do for yourself, but it is also probably the most difficult and frustrating step to navigate in this process.

I think everyone has heard the saying "It takes a village to raise a child," and for so many of us moms, that pretty much amounts to an annoying cliché. This supposed village that we hear so much about is nowhere to be found. In this day and age, you are lucky to live within driving distance of your parents or extended family, and being a part of a neighborhood where you actually interact with your neighbors is a rarity. Moreover, our lives have become so busy, it is hard to find the time to develop and maintain relationships outside of our immediate family.

This modern-day iteration of society has pushed mothers into isolation. We are trying to raise children in a society that has turned its back on the ideas of family, community, or any shared sense of responsibility. Neighbors are strangers, you have to schedule playdates, family lives thousands of miles away from one another, schools are no longer safe zones, and everyone is too busy to interact with one another. And frankly, moms are affected the most by these current social norms because we are being forced to raise our kiddos during some of the most difficult times without the beneficial support that previous generations had.

We have been forced into believing that we alone have to carry the work of the village. And when we inevitably can't, we feel a sense of failure that is hard not to own as ours. When mothers yell out for help, we are told to suck it up and deal with it because "You *chose* to be a mom." Everyone wants to say it takes a village, but no one wants to step the hell up and be the village everyone pretends exists. Moms are overstressed, overworked, and overmedicated trying to keep up with the current pace of life, yet we are left to our own devices to cobble together much-needed support systems that we often don't have the time and energy to build, much less benefit from.

The idea of a village sounds great, but I am sure the mere mention of it triggers a thousand questions in your mind. *How the heck am I going to find time to build a village? What does that even mean? Who is really going to step up and be a part of this so-called village? Do I have to know all these people? What if I don't like the people? Oh, God, do I have to actually be social with strangers? What if my family doesn't live anywhere near me? Do I have to "officially" invite people into my village? What if people say no? I have been doing this for so long by myself, how am I even supposed to know I can count on these fictional people? And who the hell has time to run a village?*

It's okay to freak out a little if this isn't your norm because building an intentional village is going to be hard and will require you to step out of your comfort zone. And it can be a tricky thing, especially in our digital, social-media age because we seem to have lost the ability to socialize, and we are looking for a quick fix for everything. But this process takes time and patience.

I found becoming a mom to be one of the most isolating things I ever experienced. Throughout pregnancy, it felt like everyone was congratulating me, praising me, asking me if I needed anything, almost to an annoying level. After the baby was born, people wanted to come by and see the baby for about the first month. Then, *poof*. Everyone disappeared, and I was left crying in a rocker with cracked and bleeding nipples, staring at the pile of diapers and burp clothes taking over my house, watching my husband still going to the gym, wondering what the hell did I get myself into—and where is this damn village?

The first time I saw the true impact of having the support of a whole village was when my firstborn had open-heart surgery at only eight months old. As you can probably guess, my husband and I were terrified. We literally and figuratively clung to each other as we dealt with the news and impending surgery. On the day of the surgery, so many of our friends and family showed up to hold our hands, laugh, talk with us, and bring us food. Honestly, my mind draws a blank for much of that day, but I do remember the friends and family who showed up for us and helped us make it through. I knew that *that* was the kind of support I not only wanted but needed.

Over time, I have managed to build an amazing village that works to support me as I walk through this parenting journey. I built my village brick by brick, and it has taken an investment of time, energy, some hurt feelings, and extroverted tendencies that I don't really have to spare. I had to build relationships, cultivate friendships, think out of the box, and be the village I wanted for myself. Was it hard? Yes! Did I have to step out of my comfort zone? Yes! Did I make mistakes and lose some people in the process? Yes! Do I regret any part of it? No!

The village I have to lean into now is worth every minute, every disappointment, and every ounce of discomfort. I have created a robust and reliable system of people, places, resources, services, and more. And if I had known what it really meant to raise kids as the primary parent, I would have started consciously building my village from the moment I found out I was pregnant, because now I feel part of a village that accepts me, flaws included, and I am more connected, supported, and secure than I was even before having kids.

As the mom, you tend to be the primary parent and carry the heavier load of parenting, and you need all the support you can get. I think recent times have really highlighted how unbalanced the scales of child-rearing are, and so many mommas have hit a wall. And if you are anything like I was, the burnout you are facing is pushing you to reevaluate how you have been approaching this whole parenting thing and looking at all the people, places, and resources around you to step up and help so you aren't carrying the load all by yourself.

But before you start building your village, you need to make a very important shift. If you want to start unloading your plate and handing over responsibility, you must be open to not being the one doing it all and being okay with people doing things their way—that is, you need to heal from Super Mom Syndrome. I know from experience that is easier said than done. When you have been the one running the show, it often feels easier to just do it all yourself because people don't do it right anyway, or people tend to disappoint you, or you just don't feel safe letting people in. I admit that I had to do a lot of internal work to get over Super Mom Syndrome and be able to let go of the martyrized idea that I had to be the one to do it all or it wouldn't get done the way it's "supposed" to get done because, at the end of the day, "Done is better than perfect."

Now, last but definitely not least, I need you to hear me and hear me good when I say this: You don't need to be perfect in any way before you start building your village! You don't need a better house or apartment. You don't need to lose weight or get your prebaby body back. You don't need to put away laundry, clean your kitchen, or replace the stained carpet. You don't need a better wardrobe, and you don't need to worry about looking like you've got your shit together. All you need to do is show up as your whole, flawed self and get to work because none of us have it all together and if we did, we wouldn't need the damn village in the first place. Now read that again—and then again—and as many times as you need to do so to get it through that stubborn little head of yours!

The Village

The gag is that mothers have been set up to believe they should be able to do it all, but the bullshit idea of balance was never meant for you to achieve on your own. You see, in order for you to feel balanced, someone or something has to counteract the weight that you are carrying. The very definition of balance is an even distribution of weight enabling someone or something—*you*—to remain upright and steady. And you need a village with the people, places, resources, and so on to offload responsibility onto so that you can remain emotionally, mentally, physically, socially, and spiritually upright and steady.

So where do you start? By building out the pieces of your village based on the reality of your life. Your parenting journey is different from every other parent's, so your village will not look like anyone else's. Yes, we all share commonalities, but no two people have the same kids, family structure and dynamics, coparenting arrangements, social network, budget, access to resources, level of health, day-to-day life, and so on and so forth. You have to build the village that works for you and includes the people, places, and things you need and want in order to feel supported in your journey.

The good news is that you probably already have all the pieces surrounding you that you need to build a village. It's just that you have likely overlooked them because you are spending the majority of your energy just surviving your days. So, a great first step is to start shifting your perspective to begin to see everyone and everything that touches the life of you and your children as a potential source of support. This can span from the people occupying the same house as you to your extended family, your friends, the schools your kid(s) attend, the neighborhood you live in, your workplace, your medical insurance—and even down to the apps on your phone.

The unfortunate part of this is, yes, it is up to you (once again) to break this super mom stigma that has been placed on your shoulders and build your own village. As the saying goes, "If you build it, they will come." The more you grasp on to this concept, the more aware you will become of consciously incorporating all these pieces into the network of your village. And as you begin to piece together the puzzle and strengthen your structure of support, you will begin to feel relief from the amount of stress and pressure on you.

And don't you dare feel one ounce of guilt for asking your village to start stepping up to support you more. Raising children to be well-adjusted, capable adults is a key part of creating a functioning society, so you should not feel guilty about calling on a parenting partner, family members, workplaces, government, schools, services, or others to step up to the plate and support you. Children become the adults who make up our society along with everyone else—participating and benefiting together. No matter what society will have us believe, mothers should not be the only ones expected to bear this heavy load.

You and Your Parenting Partner

First and foremost, your village should center around not just you but you and your parenting partner—your husband, wife, boyfriend, girlfriend, ex-husband, ex-wife, baby daddy, baby momma, whatever you call the person who is supposed to be parenting with you. Yes, both of you! Not you at the center and then your partner on the peripheral waiting for you to ask for help before jumping in (although I know that's the functioning dynamic for many mommas). This may be easier said than done for some, but the last thing an overwhelmed mom needs is a partner who needs to be managed like a child.

Ideally, every mother should be able to be in a reciprocal partnership with their parenting partner, no matter the relationship status—married, divorced, single, or it's complicated. However, I know that not everyone is able to have an active parenting partner. Unfortunately, you may just need to accept your truth and move on because it is a safer or healthier option for you and your kid(s). Whatever your circumstances, I want to again acknowledge how challenging a position this puts you in and the extra toll it takes on your time, energy, and overall well-being.

I want to say how unfair it is that you have been left to do all or the majority of the parenting without the support of an active or co-operative partner. If your partner has chosen not to be an active part of their children's life or to make your role as their mother as difficult as possible, that is a reflection on them and not you. Don't be embarrassed by that. Be proud of the fact that, no matter how hard it gets, you show up every day and try your best to provide for all your kids' needs. Take a breath and move on to the next section.

Now, even if you have two relatively emotionally mature and mentally healthy adults, parenting with another person is challenging to navigate whether you are in a relationship with them or not. Every person comes to parenting with their own familial background, perspective on parenting, ideas around discipline, expectations, and all the baggage of their childhood trauma. And the truth of the matter is both of you will never be 100 percent on the same page, 100 percent of the time. You will disagree, you will have to compromise, and there will be times you get really frustrated with your parenting partner. But raising kids should always be a collaborative process based on reciprocity: That is, you got each other's backs even when you don't like each other very much.

Furthermore, I think it's fair to say this generation of parents is navigating big shifts around the traditional roles of men and women. The domestic labor of raising children and the mental load that comes with it have historically landed on the shoulders of women. But today's requirements of running a household and raising children are very different from what they were just a generation ago, and women are asking men to step up. The times are a-changing, and some men need to catch up to the fact that providing financial support and protection is no longer enough.

This is not about making the division of labor equal, because it's nearly impossible to make things fifty/fifty, all the time, in every parenting dynamic. This also isn't about whether you are a stay-at-home mom, working mom, work-from-home mom, or any iteration in between. It's about not feeling alone in raising your children and creating a situation in which both parents feel heard, seen, supported, and valued. This topic alone could be a whole series of books, but right now let's start with a few things that can be done to create a more supportive relationship with your parenting partner regardless of your current relationship status.

Communicate, communicate, communicate. I can't say it enough, because if you and your parenting partner are not communicating with each other, you will be destined for years of strife. You have to be in conversation about the big things—like the values and morals you hope to raise your kids with—right down to the most mundane, everyday things, like who is picking up who from where. The important thing to note is that healthy communication is not always about agreeing but it *is* about a two-way street that is not only about talking but also actively and openly listening to the other person. And basically, everything comes back to the need to be in constant communication with your parenting partner.

No, it isn't always easy. There will be miscommunications, you will disagree, you won't like each other sometimes, and there won't always be common ground to be found. And, yes, it is absolutely normal to feel inordinately angry at times and flip your partner off behind their back or have irrational, violent urges (like throat punching) flash before your eyes that you should absolutely never act on. What you can do is

- Keep the needs of your children at the center of your decisions and interactions.
- When there is a conflict, focus on the issue at hand and avoid personally attacking your parenting partner.
- Always treat each other with respect even when you are mad.
- Don't forget that communication also includes nonverbal cues, so be mindful of your tone and body language.
- Be willing to compromise.

Don't forget: There is no way to get around communicating with your parenting partner as you are now tied to this person through your children for the remainder of your parenting days. So whether your parenting partner is your favorite person on earth or the most infuriating person you have ever met, you have to try your best to never assume anything, speak up for yourself, and don't shut down (unless being emotionally unresponsive, also known as "gray rocking," is a necessary tool for your safety), because these things are essential to your parenting partnership.

It is also pertinent to make sure you create opportunities to communicate with each other, like family meetings, regular check-ins with your partner, and simply chatting about your day. This is possible even if you are coparenting but not in a relationship; you just both have to be willing to be intentional about making it a priority. I know it is possible because I watched my parents navigate a divorce while still respectfully interacting and communicating with each other. And the wonderful example they set for me made it much easier for me to figure out how to peacefully coparent with my husband and his ex-wife, and I do love the big, beautiful, blended family we have created through love for the kids, respect, and communication.

Share the load. I daresay that sharing the load can be one of the most contentious parts of parenting with someone else. I struggle with bringing this up because it is such a layered topic to approach and there is no way to properly address it in just one section in a book. But it is such an important part of creating a supportive relationship between parents that it has to be mentioned.

Sharing the load is so much easier said than done because the load of parenting is so very heavy, and much of it is not even visible because it is the mental and emotional labor of raising children. For the most part, moms tend to be the ones who take it on and not because we want to but because we have been conditioned and expected to. It is so embedded into the psyche of being a mom that it seems near impossible to pass over to our partners—because we can barely articulate what it is to ourselves.

It's hard to explain that cooking dinner day-in-and-day-out can be an overwhelming task because it includes so many damn steps that you don't even realize you are doing half of them—the meal planning, the grocery shopping, the actual cooking, and navigating all of it while remembering everyone's likes, dislikes, allergies, and dietary needs. And inside your head sounds something like this:

> Let's see, we have ground turkey I need to take out of the freezer tonight for dinner, but what the hell can I make this time? The hubby would much rather I use ground beef, but I don't even eat beef and besides this is healthier for everybody, so ground turkey it is. Should I make spaghetti again because that's definitely the easiest? But the fourteen-year-old hates

> it even though it's my eight-year-old's favorite and everyone else is okay with eating it. But I did make it last week, so maybe I should make tacos instead. Okay, so whether I make spaghetti or tacos I need to pick up tomato sauce and onions and pasta if I am making spaghetti or taco shells if I am making tacos. Shit! Maybe I can make burgers instead. Nope. Don't have burger buns and we are almost out of milk. Welp . . . Gotta go to the grocery store no matter what, but when the hell am I going to make that happen? I could have it delivered, or maybe I could just pick up the groceries after soccer practice. Oh, fuck it! I'm making turkey loaf, and everybody can be mad at me.

Take this internal dialogue of emotional and mental labor and apply it across all the things. It's not just laundry: It's making sure that everyone has the clothes that they need, in the sizes that they need, for all the events coming up. It's not just bedtime: It's the backward planning of when homework has to begin in time for dinner and when dinner has to start to be done in time to get baths and showers started. And then there is managing to keep tired, overstimulated kids who refuse to cooperate on track without losing your shit because you are also tired and overstimulated and wished it all went smoothly just for one damn night.

Unfortunately, because women have been the ones culturally and societally groomed to do this work, many male partners seem to be unaware of or not capable of fully comprehending the profound impact of emotional or mental labor. This isn't a way to excuse men from the reasons they don't participate or place the burden of changing the dynamic on women. This is about opening up the lines of communication in your parenting partnership so that both of you can become aware of and work together to dismantle the culturally embedded gender norms that create this unfair division of mental and emotional labor.

The hard things I had to (and continue to) work on is genuinely asking for help, fully handing over tasks to my husband, and releasing all need to manage those tasks in any way. I had to trust that he would take care of it, release the idea of it being done my way, and refrain from being a taskmaster—in other words, I had to learn to back the hell off and let him handle things his way. And as much as I don't want to admit it, I also had to stop secretly keeping score of who did what and tallying up resentments toward my husband that he was unaware of—not at all beneficial for our relationship.

We mommas have to stop believing that this labor is our burden to carry alone, and dads need to become more aware of and more active in the day-to-day tasks of parenting their kids. The hard part about this is that you have to have ongoing, difficult conversations with your partner and be open to understanding what the division of labor looks like from both of your perspectives. I know this, because my husband and I had to do it and continue to do it regularly. And I am not going to sugarcoat it: Even when you have two willing participants, making these kinds of changes is extremely difficult. My husband and I definitely need the ongoing help of a therapist to walk us through the process, and I'd recommend it highly for anyone else.

Honestly, with these couple of paragraphs I can't even begin to scratch the surface of this part of parenting, and no way can I fully address the impact of learning to share the load—because that would need be an entire book. What I can do is recommend some really great sources that offer more of a deep dive, like *Drop the Ball* by Tiffany Dufu, *Fair Play* by Eve Rodsky, and *Releasing the Motherload: How to Carry Less and Enjoy Motherhood More* by Erica Djossa.

Be a team. Sharing the load is part of being a team, but the other side of being a team is working together to present a united front around your children, even when you don't agree. Kids know from a very young age if they can pit their parents against each other, and they will use it to their advantage without a second thought. Constantly going against each other or not supporting your partner's decisions just makes it harder for everyone involved in the long run, especially the children. Presenting a united front for your children creates a secure foundation for them to grow and develop.

It's hard to have a united front when you don't always agree on things, but as I said before, no matter how much you get along with your parenting partner, you will never be on the same page 100 percent of the time. It is good to have healthy, respectful discussions when dealing with a disagreement (that also sets a good example), but what you want to avoid is undermining each other or throwing each other under the bus. You will most definitely disagree with your parenting partner, and you will probably get annoyed or maybe even pissed off, but try to keep your eye rolls to yourself and bite your tongue if you have to until the two of you can talk in private.

The key to being a good team is to have guidelines for you and your parenting partner so that you have an agreed-upon approach when it comes to most issues that will arise. Know that deciding on those guidelines takes some negotiating up front where both parents will have to compromise. Moreover, when a disagreement comes up, you set aside time away from the kids to discuss it. Because an overwhelming number of parenting decisions come up daily, this ongoing process will require lots and lots of communication.

Lean into each other for emotional support. Nothing is more emotionally taxing than raising children. Kids will tap dance on your last nerve without a care in the world, and the next thing you know you are yelling at your partner when you are actually mad and overstimulated because of your energy-vampire kids. It is so easy to direct negative feelings like exhaustion, frustration, and anger at your parenting partner, but don't let those kids have you thinking you hate your partner when they're the ones who have sucked up your last ounce of patience.

Emotionally depending on someone else can be a very vulnerable and uncomfortable position. But knowing that your parenting partner emotionally supports you increases intimacy and trust, which in turn strengthens your relationship. But in order to do that, both partners need to know that they are in a safe and judgment-free environment. The first step is talking to your partner about how you are really feeling, because it is easy to get caught in the trap of pretending things are all good when they are not.

This is yet another very layered topic where a lot of couples need professional help. If you or your partner are not adept at emotional vulnerability, that becomes a skill that the two of you will have to work hard at creating in your relationship. That said, here are a few of the skills both partners can work on to foster emotional support in your relationship:

- *Listen to each other.* Everyone wants to feel heard—and the more we feel heard, the more we are willing to share.
- *Practice self-awareness.* Being self-aware gives you the ability to identify your emotions. It's not the easiest thing to do, but

you have to check in with yourself so that you can name the feeling. That's very important because you need to communicate those feelings clearly to the other partner.

- *Ask for what you need.* Don't assume your partner is a mind reader. Once you have identified your feelings, you can then ask for how you want or need to be supported instead of letting your partner try to guess. Sometimes I need my husband to listen to me vent without offering solutions; other times I need him to come in with the "dad voice" and back me up; and then there are times when I just need to cuddle into his lap and sniff his neck (don't judge me: I find his scent calming).
- *Validate feelings.* Celebrate with your partner when they are happy, commiserate with them when something has upset them, or just let them know you hear them when they express an emotion, even if you don't agree with their reaction.
- *Pay attention.* People usually have signals they give off when they have certain feelings. Sometimes they are intentional and sometimes they are unintentional, and when you spend a lot of time with someone, you start to pick up on those signals. Paying attention to those signals can provide you with a lot of information about where your partner is emotionally.
- *Reciprocate.* In order for both partners to feel emotionally safe, it has to be a give-and-take situation. You have to be willing to be there for your partner emotionally in the ways that they need or want you to be there for them, and vice versa.

As much as it may feel like it sometimes, your partner is probably not the enemy. Taking negative feelings out on our partners often stems from feelings of exhaustion, frustration, and even inadequacy. Allowing yourself to emotionally lean into your parenting partner can help manage stress, burnout, and difficult moments.

Prioritize time as a couple. Obviously, this one is for couples. It is easy to become so focused on parenting that you become roommates with your partner and forget that you actually like the person and enjoy being intimate with them. If you spend all your time in parenting mode, you start to shut out the intimacy part of your relationship and stop connecting with each other as a couple.

You have to make time to focus on the intimate bond between you and your partner. And it's not always easy to do, especially when you have young kids who are constantly cock blocking (yes, I said that). But you have to make the effort to prioritize the relationship, even if you have to get creative and plan dates at home or on your lunch hour. Intimately touch each other just in passing even if your kids gag every time you do it. Sext each other, emojis included, no matter how silly it feels. Chat in the bed at night for just a bit before you pick up your book or start scrolling social media. Find the ways to connect outside of being a parent that continue to fuel the intimacy between you.

The stronger your partnership as parents is, the stronger the foundation for your kids. And if any of these issues are challenging to you and your parenting partner—and I guarantee all parents will find at least one of these areas to be a challenge—don't be afraid to seek the support of a therapist. My husband and I have hit roadblocks along the way on this journey of parenting that had me really thinking twice about who the hell I married (j/k, not really, well sort of), and the support of a therapist did wonders for our relationship. And you may be tired of hearing me say it, but therapy with the right therapist really does work when both partners are invested.

Naturally, I am going to make you follow through with some concrete steps. I want you to list three changes you want to make to create a more supportive relationship between you and your parenting partner whether you are together or not. This may be having more date nights so that you feel more connected, setting aside time to talk through the logistics of the week so it's clear who is doing what, or asking your partner to fully take on a task like homework or laundry so it is no longer on your list. If you are dealing with someone who is not an active partner in any way, move to the other sections where you can focus on building supportive relationships with the people who are active in your life.

1. ______________________________

____

____

2. ______________________________

____

____

3. ______________________________

____

____

Family

Our immediate circle of people is of the utmost importance when it comes to building a village. Outside of a parenting partner, family members can be the first touchpoint for a lot of people. If we are lucky, they can be the first ones we look to for support in day-to-day life and when we are facing a challenge. Parents, grandparents, siblings, aunts, uncles, cousins, and even in-laws can be invaluable members of your village. And what better candidates for your village than the people who have loved and supported you or your partner in life before you became parents? Family, immediate and extended, can be some of the greatest support systems, especially if they live nearby. They can assist with childcare, be a place of connection or refuge, provide you with emotional support, give financial assistance, share family traditions, and be a safe space for social interactions just to name a few ways they can support you.

Even if they live far away, your family can still be a source of support—phone calls, holidays together, any way that helps to relieve the weight of the load on your plate. Not until the last five years or so did my mom, dad, and brother move within a thirty-minute drive of me (we have yet to convince my sister to make the move too). It has been great having a closer family because I have spent most of my adult life living far away from them. But I always knew that no matter how many times I needed to call my mom, she was there for me. When I fell down the stairs and tore a ligament in my ankle, my dad hopped on a plane so he could help me with the kids while my husband was away for work. My sister has come several times to watch my kids so I could get a break and spend time away. And I love having my brother and his family nearby where we can pop over and spend time together just because.

Unfortunately, in this modern world, because of geographic distance, emphasis on individualism, and the focus on nuclear-family homes, many mommas have become far removed from seeing our families as sources of community. I was sad to find that many articles about how parents can build a village don't even mention family as an option. I get that there are many reasons that parents don't have family as an active part of their village.

I am so very grateful to have my family as an essential part of my village, but I know not everyone has a healthy relationship with their family members. Family dynamics are often complicated, which needs to be considered before you decide to add a family member as a part of your village. That's right: Just because they are your family does not mean they get a spot. No, no, no! Anyone you invite into your village must be safe, respect your authority as a parent, not overstep the boundaries you set, and have good intentions for you and your children.

You don't owe anyone access to you, your parenting partner, or your kids. And if anyone is disrespecting your boundaries, you have the right to deny them access regardless of their familial relationship to you. In other words, I don't give a damn if it's your mom, mother-in-law, sister, brother-in-law, cousin, grandpa, auntie, or second cousin on your great-uncle's side. They can get with your program or step the hell aside. And don't you feel an ounce of guilt about following through on that if they continuously trample all over your boundaries.

The other part of family as a village that I realized I had overlooked is treating as a village the people who live in the house with me. I had to let go of the idea that managing and running my home was totally up to me and ask that everyone contribute. It should not be up to me to do all the cooking, cleaning, organizing, managing, and maintaining in the household, and the same goes for you. My motto is "If you live in the house, you contribute to the house." I have already addressed parenting partners; children, even at a young age, can clean their rooms, do their laundry, take out the trash, do dishes, and keep common living areas clean and organized. The older they get, the more they can do—and what better way to prepare them to be adults and be contributing members of their own households when they start their families?

List three family members and what you will ask them to do to create a more supportive village. Maybe your kids can take on more chores, like laundry or dishes. You might be able to ask your parents or in-laws to babysit once a week or so to give you a break. Or your sister, brother, or cousin can act as a safe person you trust where your kids can go for difficult conversations. These are just a few ways you can garner more support from your family. Now list some of your own ideas.

1. ____

2. ____

3. ____

Friends

Friends are the family you choose, and for so many, friends are more of a family than their blood relatives. These days, it's not unusual to live across the country from your family, so calling on your mom, dad, sibling, aunt, or uncle to give you a helping hand is out of the question. And that's where our friends can play such a vital role in our villages.

As a true Cancer, friendships are extremely important to me, and I have craved that type of community my entire life. I have always been involved in friend groups: I was a Girl Scout, I joined a sorority in high school, I was in some form of a dance company from the time I was a child into adulthood, and almost every job I have had has been either in a nurturing or community-building role. Naturally, when I became a mom, I wanted the same thing. But once I had my first baby, I realized that I didn't have the mom community I wanted or needed.

I met my very first momma friend on a tour of the hospital when we were both pregnant with our first kids. She and her husband were a stunning couple who stood next to me and my husband on the elevator. Normally, I would have shied away from speaking to complete strangers, but I got a warm vibe from them as we walked around the hospital together for the better part of an hour. We randomly ran into each other at the grocery store after I had my baby, and with one phone conversation, I was sure we were going to become very good friends.

Once her daughter was born, we were having playdates in the park, hanging at each other's house, signing up for all the kid activities together, and chatting on the phone regularly about all the new parent things when I had no one else. She bathed my children when I was too sick to sit up, and I cared for her oldest when she unexpectedly went into labor with her second child. We have been each other's backbone as we both navigated special-needs kids. She always gives me sound advice, and I am her sounding board when she feels the pressure of motherhood. I don't know if it was God, karma, or the universe that made our paths collide, but now, almost fifteen years later, she is one of the anchors in my life.

I know how lucky I was in getting one amazing friend but then, thanks to joining a mom group called Mocha Moms, I got more friends. During the pandemic, we realized that we all lived within driving distance and had kids of similar ages, so we decided to build our bubble with one another. We made a point of regularly hanging out to get social time for us and the kids, calling each other to vent about the nightmare of simultaneously managing work and virtual schooling, and we started taking escape weekends away to help us cope through all the crazy of virtual school, working from home, bitching about our husbands, and feeling like we could never get away from it all.

Having other moms to lean into during that pandemonium made me feel less crazy and less overwhelmed and thank goodness our friendship has extended beyond that time period. I now have a group of true-blue mom friends, and we are all locked in to doing life together, including a "Golden Girls" pact to move in together in our golden years. I would even go so far as to say that intentionally maintaining these friendships is one of the most important pieces of my self-care.

I know that not everyone is super social, and people aren't prone to having a huge circle of friends as a part of their everyday life—and that's okay because this isn't a numbers game. When we talk about friends, we are looking for quality over quantity because the support a true friend can provide is unmatchable. Yes, making friends as adults is hard, and when you add being a parent to that it becomes almost impossible. Busy schedules, never having someone to watch your kids, or not knowing if you are even capable of interacting with adults anymore can all get in the way of making new friends. But just one friend who gets you or is simply willing to step in when you need them can be the lifeline you need to get through the challenging journey of motherhood.

Every friend doesn't have to be your devoted bestie. There are different levels of friendship you can invest in based on your wants and needs. There are acquaintances, casual friends, work friends, and even friends of convenience. It could be a work friend who you grab lunch with because you enjoy having an adult conversation with them and you get a pleasant interaction with someone outside of your kids. Or maybe your kid's best friend's mom is pretty cool, and you guys take turns hosting playdates for the kids to give each other a break. All levels of friendships have something to offer, so there is no reason to dismiss a friendship as not beneficiary to your village just because they aren't the ride-or-die type of friend.

Regardless, making friends can be daunting, and I get that not everyone wants to put themselves out there. I could go on and on about the typical ways of making friends people usually mention, like joining mom groups, going out more often, volunteering, or becoming more active at church or your kid's school. But the truth is where you go to make friends doesn't matter if you don't cultivate the skills you need to build friendships. What are those skills? They include stepping out of your comfort zone, embracing vulnerability, communicating, and reciprocating.

Step out of your comfort zone. You aren't going to make new friends doing what you have always done, especially if you are not prone to being social. You are going to have to step out of your comfort zone and do something different. That may mean striking up a conversation with another parent at your child's after-school activity, even though it may feel awkward as hell. Or it may mean going out to more events or joining a social club like a book club or mom group that you would normally avoid like the plague.

None of this is going to happen unless you get out there and participate in the process. Unfortunately, that means you gotta go out into the world and interact with people. I know, I know. I am a fairly social person, and even I prefer to spend the majority of my time comfortably cuddled up in the corner of my couch watching reality TV while I crochet. But the more you put yourself out there and interact, the more opportunities you will have to meet new people.

The majority of the friends I've made in adulthood came after I took a chance and stepped out of my comfort zone. I can almost promise you that the momma sitting next to you at your kid's afternoon activity feels as socially awkward as you and probably would like a mom friend or at least someone to chat with just as much as you would.

Embrace vulnerability. It is hard to find friends who make you feel safe and understood—friends you can share your true self with and you know they won't judge you. But you first have to let people in and give them the opportunity to earn your friendship, which calls for you to be vulnerable. In order to build trust and strengthen bonds in your friendships, you have to be vulnerable enough to openly share your true feelings, thoughts, and experiences with another person.

Allowing someone to get to know you like that doesn't happen overnight. Start small, and as you build trust you can open up more at a pace that feels good to you. Let them hear you curse like a sailor, show them your messy house, and share about the things you struggle with in motherhood. Also let them see the fun personality quirks or weird hobbies you have, or be honest about why your partner is on your last damn nerve. You don't have to trauma dump and share all the things all at once, but open yourself up so that a new friend (or an old friend) can get to know you.

Yes, it is scary to open up, especially if you have been hurt in the past. But the best thing you can do is show your messy, unfiltered self so that you can attract the people who accept you as you are. And please know that not every friendship is going to work out for a variety of reasons, and that is okay. Not everyone you meet is going to be your type of person, but that doesn't mean you should stop trying.

If social anxiety is severely impacting your life and your ability to interact with adults outside your home, reach out to a therapist.

With that said, what three ways can you lean into your friendships to create a more supportive village for you? Is there a friend you know you can call when you need to bitch about anything, and they don't judge you? Do you have a friend or friends who you can regularly spend in-person time with? Or do you have a friend you trust enough to list as an emergency contact who would pick up your kids if needed without hesitation? If you don't have friends, list three things you are going to do to build friendships or at least get to know new people.

1. ____

2. ____

3. ____

Community

The community that surrounds us is so important to the daily function of our lives. Your neighborhood, neighbors, the schools your kids attend, teachers and class parents, your religious or spiritual group (if any), the sports teams your kids compete on, team parents and coaches, your workplace, coworkers, and more: All of these people and places are a part of your community. Each of them has the potential to provide support and contribute to the state of your overall well-being and therefore should be considered part of your village.

I know it is hard to think about support on a community level when you are in the day-to-day trenches of raising children, but finding ways to get involved and engaged in your community helps you to feel connected to those people and places and builds feelings of safety and security outside your home. Talk to your neighbors, volunteer at your kid's school, use your local library, go to the neighborhood park, or sign up for the sports programs and summer camps at your local community center. Engaging in your community helps you build connection beyond your inner circle, which makes it easier to see your community as part of your village.

List three ways you can incorporate people or spaces in your community into your village. Can you create a chat group with your neighbors to share information or even ask to borrow a cup of sugar? Is your neighborhood park a safe place for your kids to play? Are there free programs available at your local library or community center for your kids?

1. ______________________________

____

____

2. ____

____

____

3. ____

____

____

Resources and Services

A village doesn't consist merely of people or places. If you take advantage of them, resources and services can play a huge role in supporting your needs—from health insurance and access to a pediatrician to simply being able to order Instacart for your weekly groceries. An overwhelming amount of resources and services are available to alleviate some of the emotional, mental, and physical load that can weigh on you. Finding those services and resources that can help lighten the parenting load and that align with your needs—and, what's more, your budget—is also a key part of building a village.

Local county government offices offer free mental health services, learning interventions and support services for children with disabilities, and free prenatal and postnatal support, just to name a few. Library-card holders can access free tutoring services, free or low-cost tickets to local museums and attractions, and free tax and literacy classes—and can even borrow laptops, tablets, and mobile hotspots. There are local food pantries and free medical clinics, and some states offer free universal preschool.

The Internet has a wealth of resources. First of all, with a simple online search, you can find information on just about every resource or service you can possibly imagine. YouTube has how-to videos on any topic, exercise programs, and free entertainment. You can find podcasts with expert advice, learn about parenting techniques, and research any medical condition that exists. Then there is social media—which, yes, can be a tricky place to navigate with all the "perfect" moms, snarky comments, trolls, and overwhelming amount of judgy parenting advice. But if you give it a shot, you can also find supportive Facebook groups for just about anything, local pages with great information about your neighborhood or school, and if you are lucky, you may even make a couple of Internet friends whose DMs put a smile on your face.

A bunch of apps, like Instacart, Uber, DoorDash, Amazon, Poplin Laundry Service, and Task Rabbit, offer services right at the tips of your fingers. With a little scrolling and the push of a few buttons, you can have groceries delivered; dinner dropped right at your door; Christmas shopping done; laundry picked up, washed, and folded; someone to drive you to your next destination so you can get a minute to breathe; or have a local handyman come fix your clogged toilet. All of these contribute to lightening the load, giving you more of your time back, and helping you get shit done.

If you have a need, there is most likely a service or resource that can fulfill it. Offloading some of your workload to outside providers isn't a sign of failure. It's a way to work smarter and not harder. If you have access to these supports, use them.

Yes, it will take an investment of time and sometimes money, but help is out there waiting for you. I know that not everyone has a budget that can allow for access to all of these services or resources, but I implore you to not just brush it off as something frivolous when you are considering what your budget can afford and to take your time and well-being into consideration.

List three resources or services you can incorporate into your village. Is there an online support group you can join? Can you use the subscription service from Amazon or Thrive Market to automatically replenish standard household items? Does your kid's school or a community group offer free tutoring services?

1. ______________________________

____

____

2. ______________________________

____

____

3. ______________________________

____

____

Caretakers

Nannies, au pairs, babysitters, mother's helpers, and other paid caretakers are all underutilized in the village. I would also include anyone who provides in-person services like tutors, housekeepers, house managers, in-home nurses, and respite workers. Hiring a professional can significantly lighten the load of parenting and allow you to spend more of your time and mental capacity attending to your own needs or obligations. I realize this is a luxury, but if you can afford to add a service like this to your support system, you shouldn't feel an ounce of guilt about using paid caretakers. Funding and resources may be available through local government offices, school districts, or federal programs to assist with hiring caretakers.

If this is a possibility for you, list three caretakers you will add to your village to better support you. Maybe that's a tutor because your kid's math homework is way beyond your capabilities, or you have a housekeeper who deep cleans your home once a month, or you want to send out your laundry weekly to be washed and folded.

1. ______________________________

____

____

2. ______________________________

____

____

3. ______________________________

____

____

Unlikely Sources

These days we need to think out of the box and try some things that may be considered unusual. As I've said, you are on a motherhood journey that is your own, and you need to build a village with the people, places, and things available to you. That may mean that some sources of support are not where people typically look. You shouldn't dismiss a source just because it doesn't fit the typical narrative.

Your Instapot or slow cooker can be a source of support because you can toss food in it in the morning and come home to a home-cooked meal ready to eat. There are artificial intelligence (AI) apps that can research local summer camps for you and provide you with a list of options and a map of locations. Training programs for therapists, hairdressers, dentists, and more offer free or low-cost services you can use to support your needs.

Many mommas are in situations where one or more adults are part of the coparenting mix. Stepmoms, stepdads, girlfriends, boyfriends . . . all those involved with the kids are part of the village whether you like it or not. Although we have been socially conditioned to believe that your ex's new spouse or boo thing is not your ally, you have the choice to change that for the benefit of you and your family. These other people don't have to be adversaries for you to tolerate. They can potentially be positive additions to your village. This can also go for ex in-laws, unless they have anything to do with the reasons your ex is your ex.

My husband's ex-wife is a significant member of our village, and I would even go so far as to say I consider her an integral part of our family. She has lived with us on and off for the last eight years, and as crazy as that may sound, it works. I have the support of another adult in the household, she doesn't have to do day-to-day life alone (as her kids are up and out of the house), all the kids have access to all the parents in one place, and we can celebrate every birthday, holidays, and random family gatherings together.

I challenge you to identify one unlikely source of support you would like to add to your village and the task that person, place, and or resource/service can do for you. Maybe you coparent with a stepparent who can take on school pickup a couple times a week. Use an AI app to make a meal plan and shopping list for you. Maybe you can get your teeth cleaned for free at your local college's dental training program.

Growing and Maintaining Your Village

You will most likely not have every part of the village that I've mentioned—and that's okay. Like I said, you need to build the village that works for you and is actually achievable with the circumstances of your life. If that means you joined forces with one mom to do weekly carpool, called someone to vent more regularly, and automated some of your grocery shopping on a website, give yourself credit for a job well done. The point is to set up any combination of people, places, things, services, resources, and so on to help lighten your load. And whatever that looks like for you—in this phase of your life, no matter how big or small—is a damn good thing. Yes, building a village pushes you to take a step out of your comfort zone, but you have every right to call on the people, places, resources, and services around you to step up to the plate and support you in raising the humans who make up the society where all of us live, work, and play together. And I truly believe seeing ourselves as a part of a whole village is beneficial for everyone.

Imagine the relief you would feel knowing you have a reliable person who can pick up your kids with just a phone call, or a babysitter you fully trust, or a mom friend who shows up in your time of need, or a neighbor who doesn't mind walking your dog, or access to resources like after-school care, and more. . . . You don't need to feel guilty about relying on these things because they are a planned part of your support system. Ordering Uber Eats once a week or having Instacart drop off your groceries can be intentional decisions you make to ensure that you have more time to focus on your needs.

Be aware that when you invite people into your village, it has to be a give-and-take situation. You can't expect people to always be there for you and be okay with you not showing up for them. Whether it's with friends, family, your romantic partner, neighbor or any person, there has to be a mutual exchange of care, support, and interactions. Moreover, you cannot assume that people know you need help or what kind of help you need. I promise you there are people in your life who will help you, but they aren't going to mystically appear and magically do exactly what you need them to do. You have to explain your needs so that the people in your village know how they can support you.

Last but definitely not least, your village will be an ever-evolving entity, changing, growing, and sometimes shrinking over time. Most importantly, you need to embrace the importance of relying on others and let go of the idea that you can do everything by yourself. The possibility of a supportive village that helps you carry the load is out there. No, it won't just fall in your lap, but with an investment of a little time, energy, and vulnerability, you will begin to see the benefits of having the village you always hoped for supporting you.

CHAPTER 7:

ADJUST TO LIFE CHANGES: Let That Shit Go and Move On

IS IT JUST ME, or does parenting feel like a perpetual roller coaster of ups and downs with barely a moment to catch your breath between them? It constantly seems as if the moment I feel like I get a handle on things, life takes a sudden left turn and knocks me right on my ass. And why is that usually the exact moment when some random person wants to tell me, "Ohh, it gets easier." I want to karate chop them right in the throat because this shit doesn't get easier, it just changes.

When it comes to self-care, the biggest lesson moms can learn is to not get too attached to a routine and to be able to adjust as life happens, because your self-care will never be a set-it-and-forget-it type of thing. Things can go left in a split second, and you need a practice that can bend with you when you need to change things up. What works for you with one kid may not work when you have three and what you do during a more relaxed summer schedule may not fit the crazy work and school schedules you have to maintain during the school year. When something is no longer working for you, that doesn't make you a failure at it. Instead, the practice is failing to support your needs, and it is time to reevaluate and make some changes.

The truth is that life happens—or as the saying goes, "Shit happens." Some days everything goes smoothly, and then the next day life as you know it crumbles right before your eyes and you can't do a thing about it. Then there will be days you can't believe that somebody thought it was a good idea to leave minor children in your care, because you are barely functioning yourself. It's all so unpredictable even when you have the best intentions at heart.

As a mom and stepmom of eight kids, I have experienced my fair share of unpredictability. I have come to realize that the key to surviving the day-to-day chaos of parenting is giving into the fact that you don't have control at all and you have to learn to roll with the punches. The more flexible you can be, the more capable you will become at accepting whatever is going on and making the necessary adjustments to deal with whatever comes your way. Mom life, of course, changes as your kids move through growing phases—but more often than not, you have to shift minute-to-minute, hour-to-hour, day-to-day. The constant shifting can feel so overwhelming, which is usually when all the self-care practices go right out the window.

If you notice, I refer to self-care as a practice and not a routine. Why? Routines are defined as a sequence of actions regularly followed: a fixed program; on the other hand, practice is a repeated exercise that supports you in maintaining proficiency. When you practice a skill, you don't expect perfection. You can operate under the knowledge that you are learning, mistakes will happen, and adjustments can be made. When I failed with an expected routine—whether working out, journaling, or drinking more water—I would often want to throw away the whole process. But when I shifted my perspective from seeing self-care as either a success or failure to enjoying the process of practicing self-care, it became much easier to brush off when things weren't working, make adjustments, and keep trying.

Don't get me wrong, because routines like brushing your teeth, eating, showering, and bedtimes are a part of your self-care practice, and they are great anchors for adding more self-care practices. With routines, you can turn off your mind and perform them automatically. A practice is engaged with much more intentionality, something you are actively doing. The key is to view your self-care practice as a process of building, practicing, evaluating, and editing.

Building and Practicing

With the guidance provided in the previous chapters, you have done the work to build a self-care practice to start with that fits your needs and works with the ins and outs of your daily life. You have also developed tools, resources, and hopefully a village to better support you in consistently implementing your practice. Over time, you should gain a natural momentum that will carry you through even the busy and stressful periods of life when you tend to want to throw in the towel on your self-care practice—and a lot more.

Remember that building your self-care practice is not going to happen overnight. Always start with the smallest, easiest step, especially when you are just beginning to be intentional about your self-care. Master one thing before you pile more onto your plate, and I promise you that each practice will end up having a cumulative effect on your self-care. Don't feel that you have to start right away on every single thing that sounds good for you. You will get overwhelmed and shut down if you try to put on your super-mom cape and superpower your way into a fully developed self-care practice before you have built the capacity to maintain it.

To be completely honest, it has taken me years to get to a place where I feel like I am capable of managing a practice that consistently addresses my emotional, mental, physical, social, and spiritual well-being without getting overwhelmed. Did I think it was going to take that long? Nope. Did I try to start every single self-care practice right away? Several times—and I learned the hard way it doesn't work. Am I doing all of it every single day? No. Are there some days none of it happens? Absolutely! Are there times I don't want to participate in my self-care? There sure are.

As I shared before, with the suggestion of my therapist, I started with just the simple act of reading for enjoyment because that was all I could handle. And my therapist had to drag that out of me because at the time I was so shut down, overwhelmed, stressed, and anxious that I couldn't comprehend the possibility of adding one more damn thing to my plate even if it was supposed to benefit me. But I did it anyway, and as reading became embedded into my daily practice, I began to realize that I was getting so much more from it than just a relaxing moment at the end of the day. Mind you, I was only reading for about ten to fifteen minutes per day at bedtime, but the changes I started to see made me want to make more space in my life for self-care.

Over the years, I have come to understand that improving my self-care isn't just about continually adding practice after practice to my life. I quickly discovered that if I did it that way, I would end up right back at square one. I realized that to build an effective self-care practice, I had to do more than just "practice self-care." I had to stop operating under the ridiculous expectations I had placed on myself and start taking things off my plate that I had convinced myself were necessary for me to be considered a good mom. And I had to depend on the people, places, and things that make up my village to support me in the process of growing my practice of self-care.

Yes, this is the part where I remind you that you promised yourself that you would start taking your super-mom cape off and stop operating as if it is a requirement of you to do everything, for everybody, all the time. You made decisions about things you need to delegate or outsource, or to which you just have to give a flat-out no. You listed specific things you are going to ask for help with, and you created a village of support to lean into as you walk through this process. You cannot continue to build level after level of self-care if these pieces of support are not in place to make your self-care practice structurally sound.

If you keep trying to add more and more self-care attempts without building and strengthening your existing foundation, nothing is going to change. You have to build the foundation to support the practice. How should you do that? Stay accountable to yourself, focus on consistency over perfection, continually uphold your boundaries, say no, ask for help, and lean into your village for support so it won't all come crumbling down.

Evaluating and Editing

By now you understand that self-care is not a linear or static process. Life is a series of ups and downs, and you have to adjust or change as life shifts. Sometimes everything is going perfectly, and other times you need to throw the whole damn thing out the window simply because it doesn't work for you in your current phase of life. And one of the most important steps in maintaining a sustainable self-care practice is being able to recognize when you need to make changes.

We can all admit that our body or the universe can find ways to let us know when things aren't working. The problem is, all too often, mommas like you and me have become so accustomed to ignoring our needs that we are no longer capable of recognizing or identifying the signals. Our nervous systems are so overwhelmed that our bodies don't know the difference between imminent danger and one of our kids saying, "Mom!" for the 327th time that day. Then we ignore things for so long that we end up with either chronic stress or anxiety or in a perpetual state of numbness. Each can lead to a vicious cycle of irritability, inability to relax, and possibly feelings of anxiety and depression. But by beginning to be more intentional about your self-care practice, you will be able to better regulate your nervous system so that you are more capable of recognizing the signals.

Whether you are yet able to recognize it, I guarantee that your body is sending you signals. They may manifest physically with things like headaches, muscle tension, chest pains, or digestive issues. You may experience loss of appetite, insomnia, or a new nervous habit like nail biting. You may also notice feelings of overwhelm, decreased satisfaction, loss of motivation, withdrawal from normal activities, or socially isolating yourself. You—we, because I am guilty of this also—must take these signals seriously and stop ignoring the cues our bodies are giving.

When my husband and I adopted our oldest, I foolishly thought that I would easily adjust to adding one more kid to the mix. I already had two kids so what was one more [insert maniacal laugh here]. The next thing I knew, I was getting unexplained moments where I suddenly couldn't breathe. It would happen randomly during the most mundane tasks—like driving to school, in the middle of cooking dinner, or just walking the dog. One minute I was fine, and the next it felt like an elephant was sitting on my chest. I went to the doctor only to find out I didn't have a medical problem; I was having panic attacks.

To say I was shocked would be an understatement. Not only had I never suffered panic attacks, but I had always considered myself the calm one who got shit done when things got stressful. I operated under the motto "It is what it is!" But I realized that suck-it-up-and-get-it-done attitude was not really working like I thought it was. It was a very clear sign I needed to make some adjustments to how I was caring for myself or I was going to end up institutionalized.

And you would think I would have learned my lesson, but I still tend to ignore physical symptoms to this day—and that's usually when a greater power steps in to make it abundantly clear that I need to start slowing down and doing more to take care of myself. I shared that this happened after the pandemic when I kept ignoring all the physical signs that I was burned out. I refused to pay attention to the signals and slow my ass down, and within a month my dog died, my dad was admitted to the hospital, and I fell and severely twisted my ankle, ending up in a boot for six weeks. And if you remember there was a very similar series of events right before my passport office meltdown. You can call it what you want, but I am sure that the universe, energy, God, Allah, or karma was using these events to give me all the signals that I was doing too much—and I am betting that some version of this has happened to you at some point in your life.

When your self-care practice isn't working, the signals start out small, but if you don't make changes they get bigger and bigger over time until we start to feel overwhelmed. This is usually when we tend to say, "I don't have time for this shit!" and the self-care practice goes out the door. But I implore you to start paying attention when things seem to be going haywire and take the time to reevaluate and edit your practice so that it better serves your changing needs. Yes, it takes time and patience to figure out what's not working, why, and what changes need to be made, but I promise you it is worth it to build on the work you have already done and continue prioritizing your needs.

Identify What's Changed

Any season of motherhood is full of expected and unexpected changes that can be big and small: new baby, traveling, change of job, shifting to the summer schedule, a death in the family, a kid home sick, mental or physical health crisis, partner's work schedule changes, change in relationship status, a big move. So many things can and do happen in life that require you to make big and small adjustments. Sometimes, especially when they are minor, shifts are easy to overlook. The key is to take the time to clearly identify what is happening.

Ideally, you want to be regularly checking in on your self-care practice so that it never gets to the point where you are feeling overwhelmed because it is no longer serving your needs. And you should make preemptive shifts in your self-care practice when you know things will be changing in your daily or long-term life. The reality is you have to build that skill over time as you become more attuned to your needs. But when you find that any part of your self-care practice is not working for you, you need to consider your current life circumstances and think about what changes may have occurred or are occurring that are affecting you. This step is basically reevaluating your SWOB analysis (see Chapter 3). Has a new strength or weakness developed due to changes you are experiencing? Have you lost or gained an opportunity? Are you facing a new barrier? Here are a few scenarios you may need to think through when your self-care practice is no longer working for you:

A shift in your work life. Did you start a new job or get a promotion? Did you unexpectedly lose your job? Did you quit? Do you have a plan for what is next? Are you pursuing a career change? A positive or negative shift in your job or career status can be a big, stressful change. You could be adjusting to new responsibilities and more demands on your time if you have a new job or promotion. If you have lost or quit your job, you likely have a lot of stress and worry around what comes next and changes in your finances. Pursuing a new career path can bring a whole new set of worries.

Relationship changes. New romantic relationships, breakups, changes in familial relationships and family dynamics, shifts in friendship—whether good, bad, or just hard—any of these can alter what you need from your self-care practice. You may be happy and need to let some practices go or you may need a little extra TLC for yourself while adjusting to the changes.

Changes in your mental or physical health. Whether temporary or long-term, physical illnesses, injuries, mental health challenges, new diagnoses, and more that can happen with you, anyone in your home, or even extended family can have a profound impact on you. The stress of dealing with anything from the stomach flu to perimenopause to a life-threatening diagnosis will put you in a position to either temporarily or permanently change how you address your self-care.

Change of living environment. Moving, changes in your home environment, kids moving off to college, kids moving back in after being out on their own, moving to a different locality (city, state, or country), renovations, or construction: All can cause shifts. You may have to adjust to living where you don't have friends or family, you may not have as much personal space as you did before, or you may be trying to navigate parenting an adult child living in your home. And if you are facing any of these things, you probably need a little more "whoosah" in your life.

Shifts in responsibilities and roles. Perhaps you're adding a new baby to the family, becoming a caregiver for an aging parent, getting a pet, or shifting into being a stay-at-home mom or a work-from-home mom, or going back into the workforce. As your roles and responsibilities change, your self-care has to adjust to support you in those new roles.

These are some major things that so many of us could face, but tons of random things can also pop up and throw you out of whack. Your car breaks down; your washing machine stops working; the dog gets sick; your kids don't have school, but you can't get the day off; stressing about an upcoming IEP meeting with the school for your neurodivergent child. Any combination of stressors—big or small, expected to unexpected—can create a situation where you need to reevaluate your self-care practice.

Assess What's Not Working

Once you have identified the stressor(s) or challenge(s) you are facing, you need to assess how these changes are making you feel in reference to the part of your self-care practice that is no longer working for you. This will help you know what kind of adjustments you need to make in your practice.

You're overwhelmed. If the idea of doing a particular self-care practice makes you want to crawl into a corner, some part of the practice must be too big of an ask for you at this time. What that means for your practice is that you need to find ways to simplify it, pare it down, or remove the mental load.

I wanted to take my self-care practice of exercise to the next level and add weight training, but every time I went to the gym I would shut down, aimlessly wander around, and accomplish nothing. I was getting so frustrated with myself and felt like I was just being lazy until I realized I was overwhelmed by the mental load of not only planning the exercises but also researching how to do them correctly. So I canceled my gym membership, got some weights, and started doing guided workouts on the Peloton app. I am not yet weight training as much as I would like, but making that one change helped me be much more consistent. I take that as a win.

You want to do it, but you keep forgetting. You choose what seemed to be a fairly simple self-care practice like drinking water or taking your vitamins or medicine but for some damn reason, you can never remember to follow through on it. Add any form of ADHD or time blindness and staying on top of such a simple thing can seem near impossible.

The good news is that this is usually an easy fix. It just takes a little time and some patience with yourself. It usually comes down to either making a small adjustment or two to make the practice more accessible to you or playing around with the best anchor habit to stack the practice with so that your brain is more easily triggered to do the practice. (See page 70 if you need a refresher on habit stacking.) I increased my water intake just by transitioning from a water bottle with a twist cap to one with a straw lid because having the straw made it so much easier for me to drink water throughout the day. I shared earlier how I also struggled with remembering to take my vitamins and medication and discovered that putting them next to my coffee machine changed the game for me because I never forget to have my coffee in the morning.

It feels like a chore. Not every self-care practice is going to be a delightful experience, but when you reach the point where self-care starts feeling like one more annoying thing to check off your to-do list, that is usually a fairly clear sign you are doing too much. It may be time to take a temporary break from all the self-care practices you decided you "have to do" and focus on just one thing that you *want* to do.

The point is paring your practice back down so that you can re-focus on the enjoyment of caring for yourself and move away from feeling like you are just another chore on your to-do list. Think of it as a hard reset.

When I hit the point of burnout and my self-care practice felt like a bother, I gave myself permission to relish in reading smutty romance novels and not to worry about any other self-care practice. Once I found myself feeling motivated to do more for myself, I started to slowly add things back into my practice.

Your needs have changed. You have to approach your self-care practice with the knowledge that things can change at any moment, especially when you are a parent. A new job, a new baby, a mental health crisis, or a permanent change in schedules are just a few reasons you may need to change how you are approaching your self-care needs. And if you are not willing to be flexible when those changes need to happen, you are setting yourself up to be overwhelmed by your self-care practice.

When I adopted my oldest child, I refused to take some responsibilities off my plate because I had convinced myself that the weight of parenting three kids was no heavier than parenting two. The panic attacks that started happening quickly let me know that I was very wrong about that assumption. In order for the panic attacks to stop, I had to unload some of my responsibilities.

It's too rigid or too unstructured. A rigid self-care practice can take all the joy out of self-care and make it feel like a chore, whereas a self-care practice that is too unstructured makes it easy to sidestep commitments you have made to yourself. Finding the middle ground between being too strict and giving yourself too much leeway is not easy. You have to know yourself and what works for you.

For instance, I have had to come to terms with the fact that I am time blind. As such, attaching any self-care task to a specific time of the day is way too rigid for me, and I now know I will be setting myself up for failure. The flip side of that coin is that because I manage so many people's schedules, if I don't set aside time for the things I need or want to do, they won't happen. Therefore, I often attach practices to activities rather than specific times. I take my walks or work out once my kids are off to school. If my husband is home and he takes them to school, my workout starts at 7:45 AM. If I take the kids to school, my workout starts somewhere between 8:30 and 9:00 AM. That bit of flexibility allows me to transition easily between when my husband is away for work versus when he is home.

When you find yourself struggling with implementing your self-care practice, you need to get curious about what's not working and be honest with yourself so that you can get to the root of the problem.

Then and only then can you start making effective changes to your self-care practice by way of the approaches you have been learning in this book.

Revisit the Approach

I want to remind you that when your self-care practice is not working, it does not mean you are a failure or a terrible person. All it means is the way you are approaching the practice is failing you because it's not accommodating your needs. You are not going to get everything right the first, second, or maybe even third time around. When you hit a wall in your practice, don't beat yourself up and toss your self-care out the window.

Recognize that it's time to get curious about what changes need to happen in your practice to better fit the needs you are trying to address. The goal is to set yourself up for success, whether that includes making adjustments to practices you already have in place, choosing completely different practices to replace ones that are no longer serving you, or focusing your efforts in particular areas of your self-care. It may also mean that you need to readdress the approaches of setting boundaries or building out the support system of your village.

Readdress Areas of Self-Care

Ideally, a well-rounded self-care practice address all areas of self-care: emotional, mental, physical, social, and spiritual. That is the goal you should be working toward. However, shit happens, and sometimes you need to be a little more particular and focus your energy on a few areas of self-care.

If you just had a baby, you need to focus on allowing your body to physically heal from giving birth and allowing yourself the mental support you need to help you adjust to what it means for you to now be responsible for this little person who is completely dependent on you. That's not to say you do nothing in the other areas, but working out or scheduling a girls' night is moved to the back burner. If you are going through a breakup, you are going to need to focus more self-care practices on supporting your emotional health as you heal and transition to being single.

As I was recovering from clinical burnout, I had to focus my self-care practices on my mental health. That meant going to therapy once a week, setting aside time to do the homework my therapist gave me, practicing asking for help, and being more present in my daily life. That shift in my self-care focus took about eighteen months, but trusting the process made it so that I was able to fully recover from burnout and get back to working on a well-rounded self-care practice.

ReSMARTify Your Practice

Sometimes the approach you need to take is adjusting the self-care practices you already have in place. If you find yourself experiencing overwhelm, forgetfulness, or avoidance in your self-care practice, the first thing you should try is getting even SMARTer about your practice. What does that mean? You need to check in with how specific, measurable, achievable, relevant, and time bound your practices are—or aren't.

Specific. Did you get too specific or not specific enough when setting a self-care practice?

Measurable. Is the measurable amount of time you decided to use for your self-care practice working with your circumstances?

Achievable. Is your self-care practice still achievable with the current circumstances of your life?

Relevant. Is your self-care practice still relevant to your needs?

Time bound. Does the particular time you bound your self-care practice to still work with your current availability?

Let's look at a couple of examples:

Maybe you have decided to pursue your dream of going back to school, but the reality of a full course load and going to school three nights a week is unexpectedly kicking your ass, and you are realizing that kind of commitment isn't achievable at this point in your life. But that doesn't necessarily mean you need to quit school. You could pare it back and try taking one class per semester, one night a week. You can still pursue your dream, just on a different timeline that better accommodates the current circumstances of your life. That's okay.

Maybe you decided to use weight training for your workout, but you realize that coming up with your own workouts is overwhelming and you feel uncomfortable in the gym. You may need to get a little more specific with your practice and switch to a gym that provides guided weight training like Orange Theory, a CrossFit gym, or a bootcamp.

Redefine Boundaries

Your self-care practices may be as SMART as they are going to get, and what you need to do instead is reevaluate your responsibilities so that you can redefine what you must do versus what you can delegate, drop, or outsource. You want to make the space in your life to implement the self-care practice you want or need. If you are struggling with too much on your plate, you probably want to start with this approach.

Maybe you are experiencing a significant shift in your responsibilities because you have a new job, you started caring for an aging parent, or your child got a diagnosis due to a medical issue or learning disability that requires you to do more. The reality is you will have to make choices so you can reevaluate what your new must-dos look like based on your new responsibilities, and shift some of them over to either delegate, drop, or outsource. So you have to ask yourself, what will you start saying no to, and who or what in your village can be there for you for your delegating, dropping, or outsourcing?

Utilize Your Village

As I said before, your village can be one of the most important parts of your self-care practice. A village can provide you with multiple layers of support that allow you the ability to build a self-care practice that fully sustains all your self-care needs. And it is really important for you not only to keep building out your village with the right people, places, and things but continuing to use your village as your life grows, shifts, and changes.

This biggest challenge I see when it comes to reevaluating and editing a self-care practice is that as our responsibilities and self-care needs shift and grow, we become stagnant in or reluctant to trusting, utilizing, or expanding our villages. Mommas tend to fall back into the habit of trying to do it all themselves over and over and neglect to even think about a village as an option.

Keep communicating and sharing the load with your parenting partner. Keep asking your children to contribute to the household with age-appropriate chores and responsibilities. Call on your family to help you in whatever way they can. Cultivate your friendships and allow your friends to be there for you. Look to your schools, libraries, and community centers as sources of support and resources. Hire a nanny, pay for a weekly laundry service, and have your groceries delivered to the door without an ounce of guilt.

The one thing that is guaranteed in building a self-care practice is that it will fall apart multiple times. You have to get comfortable walking through those changes without giving up on yourself, because most of the times when life does fall apart, it's not even you messing up. It's just life lifing. Life is going to throw you unexpected curveballs, and the more you practice recognizing or admitting when your self-care isn't working and making the necessary changes, the faster you will be able to let that shit go and make adjustments so you can move on to happier, less stressful times.

CHAPTER 8:

HAVE GRACE:
Congratulate Your Damn Self Because You Are the Shit!

I HAVE COME TO DISCOVER that my default setting is to notice all the things I get wrong, and I have no problem punishing myself for what I see as my "failures" as a mom. I have denied myself care because I genuinely believed that I didn't deserve downtime because I wasn't successfully caring for others. I'm not sure if that is just human nature or some terrible habit I picked up along the way to becoming a mom, but it is unusually cruel. So, as part of my self-care journey, I realized it was necessary to consciously celebrate my achievements no matter how big or small they may seem and give myself more grace in my daily life.

In the past, I fell into the trap of believing that if I didn't get everything right, then I didn't deserve to believe I was doing anything right at all. Any one negative thing that happened could immediately override the fifteen positive things that happened that day. But why did losing my cool at bedtime even though I had managed to patiently navigate parenting all day suddenly mean I was a terrible mom? Why did me forgetting one doctor's appointment after managing the schedules of four very busy children suddenly mean I was a disorganized mess? Why did forgetting to give my kiddo a glass of juice he asked for after cooking, serving, and cleaning up a meal mean that I was forgetful and neglectful?

Once I became aware of how ridiculous my self-expectations had become, I had to ask myself, *Why was I doing this to myself? How did I become my own worst enemy*? And I know I am not the only mom who struggles with this, because moms have been conditioned to believe nothing is ever good enough. Your house can always be cleaner, the meals you cook should be healthier, every free moment you have should be used to spend even more quality time with your kids. You should be more available to your family and be just as dedicated at work. You need to be skinnier, sexier, and stronger and do more face masks and red-light therapy and learn better makeup skills so you don't look your age. Ugh!

Then God forbid you take credit for anything you do right because someone will be quick to point out you shouldn't get a pat on the back for those things because they're just part of being a mom. And when we actually do something anyone deems worth celebrating, we tend to downplay the accomplishment, give credit to every other person involved, or act as if the accomplishment was a random brush of luck. And what right do you have to celebrate yourself when you still have 535 e-mails to read, four doctors' appointments to make, ten missed text messages, summer camps to schedule, a birthday part to plan, a parent-teacher conference to schedule, three bags in your trunk to take to Goodwill, two loads of laundry to fold, and so on and so forth?

Well, guess what? You're never going to get all of it done. There will always be something to do. You know how people say, "Give people their roses while they can still smell them"? This goes for yourself. What are you waiting on? 'Til all the laundry is done? All the dishes are done? The house stays clean? 'Til they are in preschool, grade school, middle school, high school, college? 'Til you catch up on sleep? Lose weight? 'Til, 'til, 'til . . .

As women, we have also been trained and socialized to quietly labor to ensure that we fulfill all the expectations made of us before we care for ourselves. And we have done such a good job that we have mistakenly made it look easy and now carry the heavy burden of "invisible labor." Doesn't everyone deserve a little acknowledgment now and then, even for the mundane everyday tasks that are taken for granted? For moms, it can feel like so many things that you do for your family go unseen and underappreciated, which can quickly lead to resentment.

What would happen if you did outwardly congratulate yourself more, more openly patting yourself on the back for all the menial care tasks you do day in and day out? What if you announced when you are planning for things like trips, summer camps, birthdays, and holidays? What if you intentionally congratulated yourself and made your labor more visible?

You deserve to be celebrated now. You should take credit for your achievements now and not after you are done raising your kids. You are allowed to and absolutely should brag about your accolades. You can pat yourself on the back for doing even just what is expected of you. You can openly acknowledge all the little tasks you do throughout your day that nobody else seems to notice.

Now read that at least three more times.

I know it is difficult to shift from constantly criticizing yourself to actively acknowledging what you are doing right. This change of perspective will not happen overnight, but it will have a profound effect on your psyche. You probably have no idea how much more you are focusing on the things you do wrong than acknowledging what you do right. Yes, you will make mistakes daily, multiple times a day, and you will have some epic parenting failures, but that doesn't make you an overall failure as a mom. You are human and therefore imperfect, which means you need to find a way to acknowledge your strengths and accomplishments as much as or even more than your shortcomings and failures and you need to be able to celebrate wins even in the face of "failure."

Celebrate Yourself

I didn't realize how much I struggled with praising myself and accepting praise from others without finding a way to dismiss it. A very negative voice lived in my head that thrived on constantly reminding me of all my failures and shortcomings. That voice still lives there, but I have managed to drown out most of the bullshit it tries to convince me of by actively praising and celebrating myself. Here are the ways I began to intentionally praise and celebrate myself. I encourage you to use these in your life to push the negative in your head to the back of your mind.

Practice positive affirmations. It may sound corny, but positive affirmations really do work. Pick statements that really resonate with you and counteract the things that the "Negative Nelly" in your head regularly says about you. Post them as the background photo on your phone. Keep a list on your bedside table. Put stickies up on your closet door or bathroom mirror, and in your car. Keep a list of affirmations on a notes app on your phone. Put them everywhere you can think of, and read them aloud as often as possible so you constantly remind yourself that you are enough, you are capable, and you are doing your best.

Correct negative self-talk. You must actively correct the voice in your head that constantly critiques you, undermines you, and is just flat-out cruel to you. Any time that bitch in your head belittles you or hurls a hurtful insult your way, I want you to catch her (aka yourself) in the act and counteract with a positive statement. When Negative Nelly tells you, "You are a hot damn mess, and you need to get your shit together," you look yourself in the mirror and tell her, "I have a lot on my plate, and I am doing my best." In other words, practice speaking kindly to yourself out loud.

Write down your achievements. I used to have a bad habit of laying in my bed at night and reviewing all the things I did wrong that day. That would usually kick-start at least forty-five minutes of my brain going through a hundred different things I needed to do to be better the next day, and then I would fall into a restless sleep. Instead, I started keeping a brain-dump notebook on the side of my bed, and at the end of the day I would write down at least three things that I achieved that day, add a couple random to-dos floating around in my head, and then read my smutty book and float off into a much more peaceful sleep. Whether you put the notebook on the side of your bed or carry it with you throughout the day, write down the things you get right no matter how small or big and see if it helps you start to change your perspective.

Reward yourself. Sometimes your efforts deserve to be rewarded, which you can do in small or big ways. It can be as simple as buying yourself flowers, a new book, or a tube of lipstick when you reach a new goal. You can treat yourself to a day at the beach, a hike with friends, or a picnic in your backyard after you survived a season of your kid's sport team. Maybe you have been literally working your butt off in the gym and have lost a few pounds and deserve a nice massage. Or you can celebrate a huge milestone in your marriage with a nice trip for you and your partner.

Celebrate with people who celebrate you. It's no fun when you want to celebrate yourself and the person you tell doesn't celebrate you back. It's hurtful and makes you feel like you should just keep things to yourself. But you just need to find the right people to celebrate with. Maybe it's your husband, who gushes over you, or your mom, who makes you feel like a big deal, or friends who will go on and on about how amazing you are. Your awesome coworker might tell you how they always knew you were capable, or your boss tells you, "Job well done." Maybe your toddler will jump up and down and say, "Yay, Mommy!" or your dad will gush about how proud of you he is. Take all the celebration you can get from the people who will give it to you.

My hope is that you not only celebrate the big wins but that you also start doing things like give yourself kudos for knowing where everybody's stuff is in the house instead of beating yourself up for the mess you haven't cleaned up yet. I want you to acknowledge the wizardry you possess that makes you capable of puzzling together school and extracurricular activity schedules instead of calling yourself a hot mess because you tend to run late. Scream out a little "Woohoo" when you get everyone where they need to go whether they are on time or not. Throw yourself a dance party for being able to emotionally regulate yourself through the chaotic witching hour with tired, overstimulated kids. And don't be above making everyone give you a round of applause when you put a cooked meal on the table at the end of a long day because that was some hard-ass work. And allow yourself a moment to crash on the couch—without an ounce of guilt—and enjoy your favorite snack after barely surviving through a shitty day.

Celebrating your achievements, no matter how big or small, is something that feels good. It reminds you to take a step back and see the bigger picture and not get mired down in the muck of motherhood. It is easy to get stuck on what you didn't do, but taking the time to celebrate your achievement is a form of self-care that many of us mommas need to practice on a much more regular basis.

Practice Grace

Now that you are on track to celebrating yourself more often, let's talk about grace. I often hear the phrase "Practice grace," but outside of a religious practice, I didn't know how to apply that to myself in my daily life. So many times I have heard the phrase "Give yourself grace," and every time I think to myself, *What the hell does that even mean?* Grace is such a big word that can't be reduced down to a single action. So what can you actually do in order to practice "grace"? What does that look like in practice?

I realized that practicing grace was really about making daily choices to interact with the world and myself with courtesy and goodwill. That doesn't mean I disregard my mistakes, but I give myself space to make mistakes and confront my reality with acceptance and kindness. It is really about slowing down and being mindful about how we interact with ourselves and others. Think of it as giving people, including yourself, the benefit of the doubt.

Grace isn't about being "perfect." It's about giving yourself permission to show up, be human, acknowledge that you're doing your best, and keep trying. Here are practical ways to treat yourself with grace and implement them as you navigate the daily trials and tribulations of motherhood.

Let go of what you can't control. Life can be unpredictable, and there are so many things we just can't control. Parenting is truly a roller-coaster ride, and a lot of the time you are hanging on with all your might just to make it through the day. Learning to let go of the things we cannot change is an act of goodwill toward ourselves that many of us need. Don't hold onto things so tightly that you get stuck in a negative space.

A big part of this is acceptance of what is. You can't control how your partner parents. You can't control your toddler's tantrums. You can't control your teenager's attitude. You can't force your mother-in-law to accept you. You had no choice in whether your child was born neurodivergent or medically frail. You can't control the economy, the cost of living, or the job market. Don't punish yourself for things that are out of your control, and try focusing on the things you can control.

I know this is easier said than done, because usually when we feel out of control, one of the first instincts we have is to assert some type of control in some type of way. Pretty much the only thing that you have total control over is yourself. You get to decide who and what you interact with, you get to define the boundaries you set for yourself and others, and you get to choose how you react in those interactions.

Practice gratitude daily. If you start from a state of gratefulness, it is much easier to act with grace. Being grateful shifts your perspective and allows you to function from a place of goodwill because you will give people more benefit of the doubt. It shifts you from a mindset of lack and reminds you of all the things that you have.

Genuine gratitude involves showing appreciation for the people, places, things, and more in life that are meaningful or valuable to you. Acknowledge the people who bring goodness into your life and share your gratitude with them. Let them know you appreciate what they do even if it's for the smallest of things. Become more observant in your day-to-day life of the things that you appreciate, make you happy, or make life easier because gratefulness begets more things to be grateful about.

Forgive and move on. Forgiveness is a gift for you, and it is not necessarily for the other person's benefit. Holding anger and resentment toward someone else affects you more than it affects the other person. Being able to forgive allows you to move on so that you don't have to carry the burden of anger or waste your energy acting out of malice against the other person. And just because you forgive doesn't mean you forget. You can let go of the malice you feel toward someone but still hold a boundary with them.

Most important, the person you have to learn to forgive the most is yourself. I don't know about you, but I am the master of beating myself up. Our own voices can be the most ruthless negativity we deal with on a regular basis. Learn to forgive yourself and let it go. You are growing and learning as a parent every day, so you need to get comfortable with messing up because one thing is for damn sure: You will not get it right all the time.

Apologize when you are wrong. You are human, and you will never be perfect, which means you will be wrong from time to time. You will be wrong with your parenting partner, kids, parents, in-laws, friends, coworkers, and more. It's okay to be wrong, and the quicker you come to terms with that, the better off you will be. It takes a lot of energy to be defensive when you are wrong, and so many disagreements go on and on simply because people refuse to admit they are wrong. Accepting responsibility for your actions and genuinely apologizing disarms people and allows all parties involved to move on.

Be mindful. As a mom, much of your time is spent in survival mode. At any given time, we have too many thoughts flitting through our minds. There is so much noise and input, and we are making a hundred tiny decisions for multiple people. The whole process is very taxing on your system and can push you to shut down parts of yourself so that you can function without having constant mini breakdowns. But then that makes it so hard to fully engage in the moment in front of us.

In order to be more engaged and mindful, practice observing your emotions throughout the day and take pauses to breathe intentionally when you need to calm your nervous system. Pick moments in the day to give your loved ones your full attention without distractions or interruptions. When facing a stressful situation like a toddler tantrum or a teenage attitude, try pausing before responding to give yourself a moment to answer appropriately.

Being mindful is not easy when you are an overstimulated mom who is struggling to stay fully engaged. But with intentional practice, more self-care, and better support, being mindful becomes easier and easier.

Have compassion. You never know what someone is going through. When you act from a place of understanding of others' suffering, challenges, or hardships, you are extending goodwill to those around you. It will then more likely be extended to you in return—and we all deserve a little more compassion. This works with your kids, your spouse, your ex, your family, your in-laws, your neighbor, and so on and so forth.

And have some compassion for yourself. Being a parent is one of the most difficult journeys with the steepest learning curves. You have to remember that both your kiddo and you are learning how to do this together and you will both make big and small mistakes along the way. The compassion and patience you show your child should also apply to yourself.

Accept people for who they are. People are who they are, and you can't do anything to force anyone to change, including your children. Accepting who someone is allows you to make a better choice about how to interact with them moving forward and releases you from the mental and emotional energy needed to brace yourself for what is surely to come.

One of my kids has been diagnosed as Level 1 on the autism spectrum, previously known as high-functioning autism or Asperger's syndrome, and parenting him can be particularly challenging. But over the years, I learned that the better I get at meeting him where he is, the easier it is to be the parent he needs. And just to call myself out, I am pretty sure that my husband wished that I closed cabinet doors, remembered to turn off lights when I left a room, and stuck to one topic of conversation at a time, but alas, that is just not how my brain works.

Interacting with others with openness, acceptance, and understanding will create healthier, more reciprocal relationships. This is especially important with your children, spouse, romantic partner, family members, and friends. The closer someone is to you, the more imperative this becomes.

Approach life with a sense of humor. We often take life way too seriously. Everything is not a dire occurrence, and from time to time a good laugh will do you better than a good cry. Sometimes things won't be funny in the moment, but you will get a good laugh at it later. And sometimes the situation you find yourself in is so ridiculous you can't help but laugh, especially as a parent. Don't forget to laugh at yourself.

Do not compare. As they say, "comparison is the thief of joy." Nowadays, social media throws images of perfection in our face almost daily, and it can be hard to not feel like you are failing. But you cannot compare your real day-to-day life to the perfectly edited one-minute Instagram reel of @TheMostestPerfectMomEver (no, that is not a real page).

If you are a single mom of three, you can't compare yourself to a mom of one with a nanny, husband, and mother-in-law at her disposal. If you are a parent of a neurodiverse kid, it would be unfair to compare your parenting to the parent of a neurotypical kid. If you are a mom who suffers from depression, it would be cruel to compare your experience of motherhood to a mom with no mental health challenges.

You are on your own unique parenting journey. I can guarantee that no one else has the kid(s) you have at the stage where they are, at this point in your life, under the current circumstance of your life, with the financial position you are in, with your current relationship status, and your mental, physical, emotional, spiritual, and social state. So don't you dare compare yourself to anyone else's journey.

Celebrating your wins and practicing grace are easier said than done. It requires you to challenge unspoken rules you have been socialized to follow and practice a level of self-awareness and maturity that is not always your natural inclination. But changing your perspective to see this as a learning process that you take on a little bit at a time versus something you are trying to perfect will help make it a smoother transition. Shooting for unattainable goals will only lead to frustration and the feeling of failure because you are unable to accomplish the picture of perfection you are holding up as the ideal.

All this doesn't mean that you shouldn't hold yourself to a standard. Of course you should have standards, and you should want to grow and learn and become a better parent. But as far as I know, no one learns very well when they are constantly belittled or made to feel that they are stupid or incapable. So I want you to list the following things:

Three things about yourself you are proud of:

1. ______________________________

2. ______________________________

3. ______________________________

Three ways you are going to celebrate yourself:

1. ______________________________

2. ______________________________

3. ______________________________

Three ways you are going to practice grace:

1. ______________________________

2. ______________________________

3. ____

____

And you can start with celebrating yourself right now because you, my friend, have completed the last exercise in this book. You have taken significant steps to build a practical, sustainable self-care practice that you can start implementing today. You can now throw right out the window the bullshit idea of balance.

CONCLUSION:
You Are a Damn Good Mom!

I HOPE YOU ARE PROUD OF YOURSELF, celebrating the accomplishment of finishing the book. Reading this book and starting the work of building a self-care practice is a huge investment in yourself. And I don't take it lightly that you chose my book to guide you through this process.

I would say, "You got this!" but I fucking loathe that statement. Why? Because people usually use that statement in response to someone telling them they are struggling. It's not only dismissive but also completely frustrating because the last thing you need is for someone to tell you, "You got this," when you absolutely do not. What I will say instead is, "You are capable of doing this!" Learning to put yourself first is challenging, especially when you have been raised and socialized to do the exact opposite. Yes, it takes a lot of work, and you will need to practice a lot of patience with yourself. It will not always be comfortable, you will get triggered, and you will want to quit more times than you care to admit. But if you commit to the process, remain open, and follow the methods outlined in this book, you will see positive changes in your life.

Your self-care practice will be an ever-evolving learning process for the remainder of your life. As you and your children get older, your needs are going to change and fluctuate, grow and shrink, appear and disappear. Remember: The key word you need to stay focused on is "practice." Unfortunately, you can't wave a magic wand over your life and fix your exhaustion, overwhelm, anxiety, or whatever else you are dealing with, but you can practice a little bit each day to get better and better at addressing your needs. There will be days you feel like you have it figured out, and other days you want to say to hell with it all.

But here's the thing: This isn't new work for you. All the things that you would like to do for yourself, you are most likely currently doing for your children. You are constantly working to plan, manage, and improve their well-being. You make sure they practice proper hygiene, eat healthy, sleep enough, go to school, make friends, get exercise, learn new things, play outside in the sun, limit their time on social media, plan playdates, celebrate their accomplishments, expose them to new things, make all their doctor appointments, teach them to set boundaries, encourage hobbies, make them drink water, teach them how to be grateful, encourage them to be kind to themselves—and after reading this book, I hope you understand the need to focus that same energy on yourself.

As I wrote this book, I have taken a bit of a trip down memory lane, thinking about my own self-care journey. And girl, let me tell you: It has been a doozy. I have cried, cursed, given up, burned out, and bounced back more times than I can count. If I can share any advice from my own experience of taking this self-care journey, it would be to keep going, keep learning, and keep wanting more for yourself.

All that aside, I want you to know you are a good mom! Yes, *you*! I know you can easily come up with a million reasons why you aren't. But I am here to tell you that there are also a million reasons why you are a good mom. And I want you to say that out loud to yourself. Go on, say it: "I am a good mom." I can't hear you, so I need you to say it a little louder: "I am a *good mom!" Okay, okay, with a little more feeling: "I am a damn good* mom!!!" That's right, you are! And every time you find your inner voice bullying you into believing that you aren't a damn good mom, look yourself right in the eyes and say it again. "I am a damn good mom!"

With all sincerity, my hope for you is that this book empowers you to stop striving for perfection and release yourself from unrealistic expectations. I hope you liberate yourself from the bullshit idea of finding balance and always prioritize your self-care. And I hope that the changes you make allow you to thrive because you feel seen, cared for, and supported not only as a mom but also as the amazing, multifaceted woman you are.

APPENDIX: Practical Ways for Moms to Practice Self-Care

IF YOU ARE HAVING TROUBLE coming up with your own ideas, here is a list of self-care practices for your reference. Some are small and some are big. Some are expensive and some are free. Some will resonate with you and some won't. You can look for inspiration or random ideas or take one idea and SMARTify it for yourself (see Chapter 3). If you are stuck envisioning what may be possible for you, read through this list for inspiration. This is simply a starting point to work from.

1. Take deep, intentional breaths.
2. Sit in silence.
3. Drink a cup of hot coffee or tea.
4. Read a book in your favorite genre.
5. Take a nap.
6. Make a delicious meal that you have been craving.

7. Start therapy.
8. Work out.
9. Take a walk.
10. Call a friend for a chat.
11. Make that doctor's appointment you have been avoiding.
12. Sleep more. Add ten minutes, add an hour, sleep for a whole eight to ten hours.
13. Clean—any part of your house.
14. Declutter and organize an area in your house.
15. Binge watch a show just for you.
16. Take yourself to the movies.
17. Take yourself on a date.
18. Write a journal entry.
19. Go for a hike.
20. Meditate.
21. Plan a girls' night out.
22. Go on a date with your significant other.
23. Just say no!
24. Ask for help.
25. Eat a nutrient-dense meal.
26. Listen to music.
27. Dance it out to your favorite song.
28. Practice grace for yourself.
29. Speak kindly to yourself.
30. Get out into the sunlight and fill up on vitamin D.
31. Celebrate your accomplishment.
32. Practice a hobby you love on a regular basis.
33. Create a self-care basket with your favorite things to keep in your home.

34. Go for a leisurely drive.
35. Take a class or workshop for something you want to learn—sewing, photography, karate—as long as it's for you.
36. Set a personal goal you would like to achieve.
37. Detox from technological devices for one day.
38. Plan your self-care practice.
39. Choose a positive affirmation to say daily.
40. Drink water.
41. Delegate a task to someone else.
42. Take a hot bath or shower.
43. Get takeout and remove the pressure of making dinner.
44. Burn a candle or incense.
45. Eliminate a commitment that doesn't serve you or your family.
46. Communicate your needs to your family.
47. Keep a notebook by your bed for nightly brain dumps.
48. Build ten minutes of quiet, device-free time into your daily schedule.
49. Join a support group specific to your needs. It can be anything from a therapy group to a local mom group.
50. Dance—in private, with your kids, or at your local salsa club. Just let your body move.
51. Actively practice gratitude. Write it down or say it aloud.
52. Get your groceries delivered. (Seriously, this is life-changing.)
53. Create a boundary and respect it. Make others respect it also.
54. Declutter your wardrobe and get rid of clothes you don't like or that don't fit.

55. Play with your kids.
56. Watch a comedy special.
57. Buy yourself a small gift for no reason.
58. Put fresh flowers in your house.
59. Invest in a planner and use it.
60. Write down what you love about yourself and post it somewhere you will see it.
61. Be creative. Draw a picture, write, sew, crochet, create a new recipe, build something, paint furniture. Get those creative juices flowing in some way.
62. Buy a fancy bra.
63. Create and practice a morning routine for before your kids wake up. For example, wake up, practice breath work, stretch in bed or while standing, use the bathroom, wash up, brush your teeth, skin care/makeup.
64. Create and practice a bedtime routine after your kids go to bed. Stretch, shower, moisturize, skin care, brush teeth, use the bathroom, read in bed, sleep.
65. Create a skin care routine.
66. Take a random day off.
67. Ask for what you really want.
68. Remove a toxic person from your life or limit contact with them.
69. Get a water bottle so that you drink more water.
70. Create a tea or coffee routine with a special mug and place where you enjoy it.
71. Plan alone time, announce it to your family, and require everyone to respect it, including yourself.
72. Clean out your purse.

73. Clean out your mom car.
74. Hug someone: a full-body-contact, tight-squeeze, lingering hug.
75. Stretch throughout your day to release tension from your muscles.
76. Take a real lunch break instead of eating on the go.
77. Connect with other moms.
78. Indulge in a delicious treat with no guilt.
79. Delegate chores to other people who live in your home.
80. Practice one small act of self-care on a daily basis.
81. Eat off real dishes—hopefully on a night when someone else washes them.
82. Get rid of an article of clothing in your closet that is never going to fit you again.
83. Buy new underwear.
84. Take a day for yourself outside of your home. Get lost in the library, lay out at the beach, have a picnic in a park, go for a hike. . . .
85. Take your medication regularly.
86. Eat fruit.
87. Eat vegetables.
88. Abstain from a vice of yours for thirty days: alcohol, sugar, chocolate, fried foods.
89. Floss.
90. Listen to a podcast.
91. Color.
92. Do something spontaneous.
93. Have sex or masturbate.
94. Find a spiritual or religious community.

95. Make a vision board.
96. Leave work on time.
97. Take a mental health day.
98. Cuddle with a pet.
99. Pray.
100. Watch a movie.
101. Volunteer for a cause that is important to you.
102. Light your favorite candle.
103. Schedule a dental cleaning.
104. Go to a performance: dance, theatre, music, an art exhibit, a poetry slam.
105. Read a self-help book.
106. Schedule a mammogram.
107. Do yoga. Take a class, find a YouTube video, or use an app.
108. Doodle.
109. Have a snack.
110. Play with a fidget toy.
111. Look at yourself in the mirror and say something nice to yourself.
112. Hug yourself.
113. Go back to school.
114. Apply for a new job.
115. Take a break from exercising.
116. Perform a random act of kindness for someone else.
117. Belt out your favorite song.
118. Reconnect with an old friend.
119. Challenge your mind by doing a puzzle, crossword, or Sudoko.
120. Join an adult sports team.

121. Pay someone else to clean your house.
122. Use a laundry service.
123. Leave him or her.
124. Start a garden.
125. Listen to an audiobook while cooking, cleaning, or doing laundry.
126. Go to a local festival.
127. Admit to a trusted person you are struggling.
128. Set a bedtime and stick to it.
129. Take your vitamins.
130. Have a good cry.
131. Make your bed.
132. Plan a trip and take it.
133. Spend a night or two at a hotel by yourself.
134. Pick a financial debt and set a plan to pay it off.
135. Join a gym.
136. Intentionally do something you don't consider productive: color, watch trash TV, play a board game.
137. Fold and put away your laundry.
138. Host a girls' night in.
139. Lock the bathroom door so you can pee or poop in peace.
140. Do ten minutes of pelvic floor exercises.
141. Stock your pantry with snacks for you, healthy or otherwise.
142. Write a bucket list of out-of-the-ordinary things you want to try: salsa class, learning another language, dyeing your hair a crazy color. . . .
143. Give yourself a hand or foot massage.
144. Roll your back out on a tennis ball.

145. Schedule a playdate for yourself.
146. Order just dessert for delivery. Yes, just dessert.
147. Moisturize your body.
148. Go for a bike ride.
149. Jump rope.
150. Hula hoop.
151. Get or give yourself a mani/pedi.
152. Write a budget.
153. Get a divorce.
154. Get a diagnosis.
155. Ask for or start that antidepressant, antipsychotic, mood-stabilizing, or stimulant medication without guilt or shame.
156. Let dinner be snacks.
157. Send yourself a postcard with something encouraging written on it. You'll get it right when you need it.
158. Change your screen saver to something that makes you smile.
159. Watch an old sitcom that makes you laugh: *Golden Girls, Girlfriends, Will & Grace, In Living Color*.
160. Try restorative yoga before bed.
161. Cancel all your weekend plans.
162. Bake something delicious.
163. Go to bed early.
164. Fire your doctor if you feel like they don't listen to you.
165. Add more variety to your diet—that is, try new foods.
166. Buy luxurious sheets and a silk pillowcase.
167. Delegate mental load task(s) to your partner: birthday planning, doctor appointments, grocery shopping.

168. Set a savings goal.
169. Talk to a minister, priest, rabbi, imam, or other spiritual leader.
170. Ask someone to be your mentor.
171. Stand up for yourself and advocate for your needs.
172. Turn off screens one hour before bedtime.
173. Ask for a second medical opinion.
174. Lift weights.
175. Add more fiber to your diet.
176. Get a facial or give yourself one at home.
177. Wear your favorite outfit.
178. Replace your old, crusty makeup.
179. Declutter your bathroom counter.
180. Watch the sunrise or sunset.
181. Use a scalp massager on your head.
182. Set a boundary to not work outside of work hours.
183. Pick out your clothes the night before.
184. Plan chores with your family so that everyone shares the load.
185. Take a day trip.
186. Call out sick when you are sick.
187. Sleep with a weighted blanket.
188. Clear your e-mail inbox.
189. Introduce yourself to someone new.
190. Travel.
191. Go somewhere fun that's marketed to kids—like mini golf, an arcade, or an amusement park.
192. Make a soothing playlist.
193. Attend a conference, convention, retreat, or workshop.

194. Go to a chiropractor.
195. Take a self-defense class.
196. Go on one-on-one dates with your kids.
197. Do something that scares you, like public speaking, dating, riding a roller coaster, or joining a social group where you don't know anyone.
198. Read a religious or spiritual text that you connect with.
199. Take a professional picture with your girlfriends.
200. List the things you are proud of and put it up somewhere you can see it.

ACKNOWLEDGMENTS

I AM BEYOND GRATEFUL for everything that led me to creating this book. Looking back, I realize there have been a series of fortunate events (even though I may not have seen them as fortunate in the moment) that led me to write this book. And there have been so many people in my life who have helped guide me to this moment.

First, I want to thank my husband, Mike, for being my rock in this chaotic journey of motherhood. Thank you for being my partner and showing up for me and our kids on the good days, the bad days, the easy days, and the hard days. Thank you for encouraging me and supporting me in pursuing my dreams. And thank you for closing all the cabinets I leave open, turning off the oven when I forget, reminding me where I left my phone, turning off the lights I leave on, and never mentioning the ever growing pile of books on my side of the bed. I love you with all my heart and soul.

Thank you to the ones who made me a mom: Roarke, Tyler, Alex, and Quincey, you guys are the best stepkids I could have asked for.

Even though I didn't know what to expect as a stepmom, you all made me feel accepted as part of the family from day one. Jackson, Nolan, Ledgend, and Davis, I hope you know that I am honored to be your mom, and I truly do consider you guys to be my greatest accomplishments. I love each and every one of you.

Thank you, Mom and Dad, for always believing in me and encouraging to me to pursue my dreams. You instilled me with a confidence in myself that has taken me so many places and helped me accomplish so many things. Karima and Sean, even though I am the oldest, I look up to both of you and greatly admire you. Thank you for encouraging me to be my best simply by being who you are.

Thank you to all my aunts, uncles, cousins, and extended family who gave me a home away from home and supported me when I was young, broke, and chasing my dreams.

Tracey, thank you for welcoming me into you and your kids' lives and being a part of creating our big, blended family. Together we have created such an amazing support system not only for our kids but for each other, and I am forever grateful.

Jeena, you were my very first mom friend and you have gifted me the most beautiful friendship. We have walked through this motherhood journey together from the very beginning, and I hope you know how much your friendship means to me. You have encouraged me from the very inception of this book, and I can't put into words how grateful I am for you. Love you, lady!

Da homies—Ify, Lia, Patrice, Stephanie, Tina, and Zandra, thank you for doing life with me. I couldn't ask for a better group of women to laugh, cry, grow, celebrate, and walk through this journey of motherhood with. You all are like sisters to me, and I love you all very much.

Steel magnolias—Christy, Carrie, Alyssa, Leah, Mary Anne, and Megan, you are the friends I never knew I needed and now I can't imagine navigating motherhood without you. I am so grateful for the safe, judgment-free space we share, and thank you so much for being the first readers of this book and giving me such valuable feedback. Love you—bye.

Swift, you are my homie for life. You have seen me through so many stages of my life, and I look forward to us seeing each other through so many more. Love ya!

April, Janisha, and Claudia, no matter how much time we spend apart, you are my dance partners for life.

Yasmine, Sagine, Yvonne, Daphne, Dana, Elke, Desiree, Jahan, Maggie, Sharon, Tammy, Vage, Dani, Sara, Tavian, Angel, Rhonda, Regina, and so many more: thank you for being my friends.

Brandi Riley, thank you for being my first writing mentor and opening doors for me that helped me land my first professional writing job. And a shout-out to all my Courage to Earn colleagues who helped give me the courage to keep going, especially Virginia, who is still my Zoom writing partner almost eight years later.

Thank you to my accountability partners Angel and Rhonda for encouraging me when I first had the crazy idea to write a book.

Thank you to Amri Kibbler and Katya Libin, founders of Hey-Mama (now known as Luminary), for giving me so many opportunities, including participating in Mama Mentors, where this book became a concrete possibility. Thank you to Hitha Palepu for mentoring me and encouraging all the ladies in your 2020 Mama Mentors group to write their books.

Kim Perel and Margaret Danko, I am so grateful to you for supporting me through writing my book proposal and pushing me to finish it. I couldn't have been more excited to be signed to Highline Literary Collective. And thank you to my agent, Amanda Bernardi, for believing in my idea and championing my book.

And thank you to Health Communications, Inc. (HCI), for publishing my book and to Darcie Abbene for holding my hand through the process of editing, designing, and publishing.

Thank you to all the beautiful moms who have touched my life in ways big and small. Thanks to all Mocha Moms of San Fernando Valley, Mothers Together, and my Soul Sistars and Debrena Jackson Gandy.

And last but not least, thank you to everyone who has supported me in any way. Thanks for reading an article of mine, liking a post, commiserating or laughing with me in my DMs, sharing my reels, buying my merchandise, signing up for my e-mail list, buying this book, and so much more.

ABOUT THE AUTHOR

ELISHA began her writing career when a photo of her breastfeeding her daughter on the toilet went viral in 2015 and she responded by publishing an article in the *Huffington Post* titled "I Drove the Internet into a Frenzy Telling the Truth About Motherhood." The article also went viral and was translated into various languages for publications around the world. She received messages from moms of all walks of life thanking her for sharing the truth about motherhood. This ignited a passion in her, and she has since published several articles for the *Huffington Post*; started her own blog, The Mom Forum; and become a staff writer for the popular parenting blog Scary Mommy.

As a birth mom of three, adoptive mom of one, and a stepmom of four, Elisha is the CEO and head laundry avoider, executive chef, chauffeur, and director of domestic operations of a company of eight. Yes, you read that right: eight kids—aka a professional mom complete with a BA in child development whose work hours are 24/7. Elisha fancies herself a self-care strategist and advocate for moms. She is a blogger of mom truth and hosted the podcast *MomCare Mondays*.

Three months after giving birth to her youngest child and enduring a string of unfortunate events, Elisha had a very public "mommy meltdown" in the middle of a passport office. After being escorted out of the room while sobbing into a cloth diaper, she realized she had to change the way she was caring for herself. A few months later, Elisha launched The Mom Forum, a blog and community supporting women in motherhood.

Elisha set out on a journey to rediscover herself and what self-care she needed to implement as a mom and wife so she wouldn't be in a perpetual cycle of losing her mind. She spent over a year focusing on her self-care practice and learning how to prioritize her own needs. She then combined what she learned with her skills as a Certified Strategic Planner and self-published *The Mom Self-Care Planner* as a guide for everyday moms to create a realistic self-care practice. After hearing that the workbook changed so many moms' perspectives on self-care, she decided to use the tools from the workbook and share more of her story in this book, *Balance Is Bullsh*t: The Truth About Motherhood and Self-Care*.

Elisha currently resides in Los Angeles, where she is raising the four kids she shares with her husband, actor Michael Beach, who happily closes cabinets behind her, locks all the doors at night, fills her gas tank, and regularly encourages her to have cackle time with her girlfriends.

Themom-forum.com

@MyLifeIsABeach